The World's
WICKEDEST
WOMEN

The World's
WICKEDEST
WOMEN

Margaret Nicholas

OCTOPUS BOOKS

To my daughters Katie and Charlotte

First published in 1984
by Octopus Books Limited
59 Grosvenor Street
London W1

© 1984 Octopus Books Limited

Third impression, reprinted 1985

ISBN 0 7064 2034 9
Made and printed in Great Britain by
Richard Clay (The Chaucer Press) Limited
Bungay, Suffolk

Contents

Acknowledgements

The publishers wish to thank the following organizations and individuals for their kind permission to reproduce the pictures in this book:
Mary Evans Picture Library 2 above, 11, 26, 49, 61, 72, 101, 105, 115, 128, 136, 170, 183, 191; Keystone Press Agency 2 centre, 123, 143, 148; The Mansell Collection 2 below, 17, 44, 52, 95, 157, 158, 167; Courtesy The National Portrait Gallery 29; Peter Newark's Western Americana 75; Topham Picture Library 81, 133, 137.

With a book such as this, covering such a wide variety of characters, the author must draw much of her information from earlier works. It would be impossible to mention all of them but the author wishes in particular to acknowledge the following writers: Betty Kelen: *The Mistresses* (W. H. Allen); W. H. Trowbridge: *Seven Splendid Sinners* (T. Fisher Unwin); Helen Holdredge: *Lola Montez* (Alvin Redman, London); Brian Masters: *The Mistresses of Charles II* (Blond and Briggs); Alyn Brodsky: *Madame Lynch and Friend* (Cassell, London); William Roughead: *The Siren and the Sorceress* (Odhams); Joanna Richardson: *The Courtesans* (Weidenfeld and Nicholson); Charles Kingston: *Rogues and Adventuresses* (John Lane Bodley Head Ltd); Judge Edward Abbott Parry; *Vagabonds All* (Cassell and Co); James D. Horan and Paul Sann: *Pictorial History of the Wild West* (Spring Books); Marina Warner: *The Dragon Empress* (Weidenfeld and Nicolson); J. O. P. Bland and E. Backhouse: *China Under the Empress Dowager* (Heinemann); Jacques Roergas de Serviez: *The Roman Empresses* (The Walpole Press); Thea Holme: *Caroline of Brunswick* (Hamish Hamilton); Henrietta Sharpe: *A Solitary Woman* (Constable); Christopher Simon Sykes: *Black Sheep* (Chatto & Windus); Margaret Fox Schmidt: *Passion's Child* (Hamish Hamilton); Margot Strickland: *The Byron Woman* (Peter Owen); Elizabeth Jenkins: *Lady Caroline Lamb* (Victor Gollancz Ltd); David Pryce-Jones: *Unity Mitford: A quest* (Weidenfeld and Nicolson); Marc Alexander: *The Outrageous Queens* (Muller); Jasper Ridley: *Mary Tudor* (Book Club Associates); Gordon Honeycombe: *Murders of the Black Museum* (Hutchinson); Gerald Sparrow: *Queens of Crime* (Arthur Barker Ltd); Arkon Daraul: *Witches and Sorcerers* (Tandem Books); Peter Hunt: *The Madeleine Smith Affair* (Carroll and Nicolson); Lord Birkenhead: *More Famous Trials* (Hutchinson); O. P. Gilbert: *Women in Men's Disguise* (Bodley Head); Arthur Vincent (editor): *Twelve Bad Women* (T. Fisher Unwin); C. L. M. Stevens: *Famous Crimes and Criminals* (Stanley Paul and Co. Ltd); Alfred Neumann: *Christina of Sweden* (Hutchinson); Ferdinand Gregorovius: *Lucrezia Borgia* (Phaidon); Clemente Fusero: *The Borgias* (Pall Mall Press); Henri Troyat: *Catherine the Great* (Aidan Ellis) also *Infamous Murders and Crimes of Passion* (Verdict Press).

Introduction

That chauvanist Rudyard Kipling once said something about the female of the species being more deadly than the male. Sometimes, as you will see, it is true. There is nothing more terrible than when the hand that is supposed to rock the cradle takes up the gun or the poison bottle. But there is also a kind of wickedness that only women can dispense. They are, when so minded, past mistresses at the art of sexual intrigue, cunning and deceit. They can manipulate with genius.

Some of the women in this book are far more wicked than others. Some were considered thoroughly bad lots simply because they behaved in a way that outraged the moral code of their times. Others were pawns in the game of life and fought back tooth and nail. Yet others took on a man's role and played it with masculine aggression.

But whether they were tyrants or killers, courtesans or queens – or perhaps just very naughty – wicked women have always proved to be fascinating, to other women as well as to men. Modern biographers tend to present them with a thin coat of whitewash but they are so much more interesting without.

Chapter
One

Mistresses

Without the mistresses of great men, history would
be very much the poorer. But some did not
hesitate to use their beauty and their power to
rock thrones, shake kingdoms and set men at each
others throats in jealous rage.

Cora Pearl

By the mid 1860's a red-haired English siren called Cora Pearl was the most famous courtesan in Paris – and the most costly. She was so rich that her jewels alone were valued at a million francs. She had three houses furnished regardless of cost, a platoon of servants and a magnificent stable of sixty horses. Her passion for luxury became a mania.

When one lover panicked at her spending she would simply move on to another until in the end she had gone through five or six great fortunes. She seldom had one lover at a time and coolly played them off, one against another, keeping a note of her wealthy admirers in a special book with a column for adding up what or how much they had given her. A young man called Duval, whose father had made millions out of hotels and restaurants, pleaded with her in a letter: 'Will you let me prove my devotion. Command me and I will die.....' She replied briefly and tartly: 'I would rather you lived and paid my bills!'

One wild extravagance followed another. She bathed in a rose marble bathroom with her initials inlaid in gold at the bottom of the bath and indulged charming little whims like serving her guests with hothouse peaches and grapes on a bed of Parma violets, the violets alone costing 1,500 francs. Her dinners, masked balls and banquets were legendary. She seldom had fewer than fifteen people to dine, so her chef insisted that he could not buy less than a side of beef at a time. One night she wagered her guests that she would give them some meat which they would not dare to cut. They waited impatiently for dinner and for the *pièce de résistance* to arrive. When it did, it took their breath away. Cora had had herself served up on a huge silver salver borne by four footmen. She was stark naked with a tasteful sprinkling of parsley!

Her extravagance seemed to spark off a streak of madness in her lovers. One presented her with a vast box of marron glacés, each marron wrapped in a 1,000 franc note. Another sent her a model of a silver horse, so heavy that it had to be carried in by two porters and was discovered to be full of gold and jewels. Prince Napoleon gave her a carriage full of rare orchids which she strewed on the floor and an Irish lover, James Whelpley, gave her his entire fortune which she spent in eight weeks.

She was certainly not born to luxury, nor with the name Cora Pearl. Her real name was Eliza Emma Crouch and she was the daughter of a Plymouth music teacher, Frederick Crouch, who became famous on his own account.

Cora Pearl

He wrote the beautiful ballad '*Kathleen Mavourneen*' in 1835, the year of her birth and she was educated on the profit from its sales.

Several years at a Convent school in Boulogne gave Cora a taste for the French way of life. By the time she returned home to live with her grandmother in London, she was a captivating young woman with rose petal skin and glorious auburn hair, only too well aware of her effect on men. She began to get bored with the steady, sober life she was expected to lead and decided she wanted to become an actress. She began to pay secret visits to the theatre. On one of these excursions she was approached by a charming, distinguished-looking stranger, who told her he was a diamond merchant. Naively accepting his invitation to dine, the inevitable happened. Rather than go back home she picked up the £5 he had left by her bedside and took a room near Covent Garden.

A theatrical speculator called Robert Bignell engaged her to sing and dance, though she had talent for neither, at the Argyll Rooms, a notorious pleasure haunt. She probably became his mistress for when he offered to take her to Paris, they travelled as husband and wife. Once in France, however, she lost no time in getting rid of him. She had plans of her own.

First she changed her name to Cora Pearl. Then she began to haunt the smart little cafés where singers were required. Managers hired her because they could see that her looks alone would attract customers. She was not particularly beautiful but had a perfect figure, glorious colouring and a kind of piquancy that made her wildly attractive.

At first she had to live in quite humble lodgings and her lovers were of no distinction. But when they became richer she squeezed every penny out of them to buy dresses from Worth and jewels from Cartier. She was a firm believer in the idea that to look successful was half the battle towards being successful. Her policy soon began to pay off.

Her first important lover was the Duc de Rivoli who not only bought her fabulous clothes and jewels but moved her into a delightful house where he paid her servants, her enormous food bills and her gambling debts. Gambling soon became an obsession and she lost money at an appalling rate. At the same time that the Duke was keeping her in luxury Cora was also giving her favours to the seventeen-year-old Prince Achille Murat. He could refuse Cora nothing. He gave her her first horse and she was so pleased with it that nothing would content her until she had a magnificent stable, tended by English grooms in yellow livery.

From 1862 Cora Pearl set the pace for the gay and elegant Paris of the Second Empire. She had started what she called her 'golden chain' of lovers. After the Duc de Rivoli and Prince Murat she added the Prince of Orange, heir to the Netherlands throne, the Duc de Morny, half brother of the

Emperor, and then Prince Napoleon, the Emperor's cousin. All of them spent fortunes on her.

Her rivals were green with envy. Some maintained that she was downright coarse and had no looks to speak of, but she retorted by asking what did it matter as she found it perfectly easy to seduce the husbands of the most beautiful women in Paris.

She would drive out in a sky blue *calèche*, lined with yellow satin and drawn by a team of *café au lait* coloured horses. Sometimes she dyed her hair yellow or blue to match. She used face powders tinted with silver and pearl and in summer stayed out in the sun to brown her skin, an almost unbelievable idea in those days of pale complexions and parasols. Her bottles of toilet water and her creams and powders were all specially sent from London though she admitted her finest beauty treatment was sponging all over with cold water every day.

The last five years of the Second Empire – from 1865 to 1870 – were dazzling ones for Cora. She had been introduced to the Emperor's cousin, the 42-year-old libertine, Prince Napoleon, who was married to the intensely devout Princess Clothilde. He fell in love with her and she soon began to demolish his bank balance. The Prince bought her a house in the Rue de Chaillot, said to be the finest private residence in Paris and rumoured to have cost two million francs to furnish. By now Cora behaved as though money ruled everything and everybody and could procure everything she desired, but Prince Napoleon seems to have genuinely wanted to please her. She had a longer relationship with him than with any other man and he was always loyal to her. On one of the nights she entertained him in her bed with its black satin sheets monogrammed in gold, she persuaded him to buy her a second house in the Rue des Bassins and to pay her gambling debts at Monte Carlo where she had lost 70,000 francs in eight months.

On 26 January 1867 she created a sensation when she appeared on the Paris stage as Cupid in Offenbach's comic opera *Orphee aux Enfers*. For one thing she was half naked, for another she wore boots on which the buttons were huge diamonds and the soles were a solid mass of diamonds. After the performance an anonymous Count offered 50,000 francs for the boots, double that if Cora was inside them.

Suddenly everything changed. In July 1870 the Franco-Prussian War began. Although it was brief it brought the overthrow of the Second Empire and the scattering of all those who had in the past decade paid, and paid dearly, to maintain her wildly extravagent way of life.

Surprisingly, Cora rose to the occasion during the siege of Paris. The pampered courtesan turned her house in the Rue de Chaillot into a hospital. She tore up her fine linen for bandages and shrouds, tied an apron over her fine dresses and worked among the wounded for 16 hours at a stretch.

Prince Napoleon, in exile, remained constant, but Cora had to have someone to take his place. Among those who paid their court to her was a young man, ten years her junior, called Alexandre Duval. He was besotted by her now mature charms and begged her to let him prove his love. Smiling indulgently she agreed. First he could pay off all her debts. And perhaps he would pick up the bill for a banquet she was planning to give.... Although Duval belonged to a very rich family owning a chain of hotels and restaurants, twelve months of Cora's demands brought the young man to his knees. When he confessed he could no longer keep up with her insane spending and that he had reached the end of his resources, she turned her back on him.

One day he followed her home and asked to speak with her. When she refused he took out a gun and shot himself. With his body sprawled on her front doorstep all that seemed to worry Cora Pearl was how society would react to this appalling business. She thought him dead and afterwards everyone remembered her lack of pity for Duval, her complete lack of compassion. Although she did not realize it at the time, her treatment of him helped to bring about her downfall.

Duval recovered from the gunshot wound but things were never to be the same again for Cora. One night when she drove to the theatre she was hissed and felt the fury of the Paris mob at her heels. Her treatment of young Duval had been too callous even for the French *demi-monde*. The affair caused such an uproar in fact that she decided it would be tactful to go on a world tour.

London did not receive her well. She had booked a suite on the first floor of the Grosvenor Hotel and paid for a month in advance. But no sooner had her mountain of luggage been deposited in the foyer than the manager, suddenly realizing who she was, quietly informed her that she must leave. It was a bitter humiliation and she had to rent a house in Mayfair at a very high price. Nevertheless, she enjoyed some triumphs in England.

She wandered about Europe for a time – Monte Carlo, Nice, Milan – making a tour of the chief casinos where she hoped to boost her flagging bank account with luck at the tables. To her fury she met with fresh humiliation at Baden where she was refused admission to the tables. Fortunately one of her admirers, a cousin of the Kaiser, saw what had happened, offered her his arm and led her in.

When she felt she had been away long enough to let the Duval affair fade in the public memory, she returned to Paris and for a time continued to give dinners and receptions paid for by admirers. But from 1874 when Prince Napoleon decided to break off his relationship with her, her life began to disintegrate.

First she had to sell off the house in the Rue de Chaillot. Her jewels went to pay her gambling debts. All her fabulous possessions were auctioned to provide money to keep her afloat. She was able to hold her own for nearly ten years but then her slide down the social ladder was rapid. She ended her career in a cheap boarding house in the back streets of Paris, her looks ravaged, her admirers, gone.

On 8 July 1886, she died of cancer. Not a single newspaper recorded the fact, the cheapest of coffins was ordered for her and a local undertaker received instructions to bury her as a pauper. Before he could carry out his orders he received a visit from a distinguished man of aristocratic bearing. 'What will the best funeral for Madame Cora Pearl cost?' he asked. Holding out a sheaf of notes he said 'The lady must have the finest funeral.' Just before he turned to go he added 'I warn you an agent of mine will be present to see you fulfil your part of the bargain.' The stranger never identified himself but Cora was buried in the cemetery at Batignolles in the style to which she was once accustomed.

Lola Montez

In her time, Lola Montez was probably the most outrageous woman in the world. She caused a King to lose his throne, set off rebellions and riots, mesmerised men both famous and infamous and stung French writer, Alexandre Dumas, into saying: 'She is fatal to any man who dares to love her.'

She was a fabulous liar, a meddler in politics, mistress to more men than she could remember and very beautiful. Her life was so crammed with adventure and disaster that one wonders how she managed to fit it all in.

Her real name was not Maria Dolores Porres Montez. It was Eliza Gilbert. Nor was she, as she so often claimed, the daughter of Lord Byron and an Irish washerwoman or, alternatively, a child of noble Spanish birth stolen by gypsies. Her background was far more sedate than she cared to admit.

Lola was born, not in Spain, but in Limerick, Ireland, in 1818. Her mother was a milliner from Dublin and her father a captain in the British East Indian Army. She was brought up in Calcutta and proved to be a wild young thing, spoiled by the attention of too many servants. When her father died of cholera her mother married his best friend, a staunch young Scotsman called Captain Craigie, who was to become Sir Patrick Edmonstone Craigie, Adjutant-general of the Army in Bengal. Lola was sent home to his Calvinist relations in Montrose, then to schools in England and Paris so that she could be properly educated and taught some manners.

When it was time for her to return and join the Calcutta set, Mrs Craigie herself came to fetch her. It was not through fondness. She had no affection for Lola. But she did have ambitions. The rich sixty-year-old Judge of the Supreme Court in India, Sir Abraham Lumley, had asked her to find him a wife. When she saw that her rebellious child had turned into a young beauty with clouds of black hair and gentian blue eyes, she felt her problems were over. But Lola thwarted her by eloping with a young officer called Captain James who had travelled over with Mrs Craigie, warned Lola what was going on, and took her back to India himself.

The charming Captain James turned out to be more interested in other men's wives and horses and soon deserted her, by which time Mrs Craigie had given up her daughter for good. She refused her financial help and thought the best thing she could do would be to go back to the good Calvinists in Montrose. But her step-father, a kind man who liked her spirit, put a cheque for £1,000 into her hand before she sailed.

Nothing would make her go back to the pious Scots, so she found herself alone in the world. She would have to earn her living. An American, who befriended her on the passage over suggested she should go on the stage. It was the turning point in her life. She couldn't act so decided to become a dancer; a Spanish dancer. Probably the fact that her mother had sometimes boasted of a drop of Spanish blood in the family, in order to make herself more 'interesting' gave her the idea. She hired an Andalusian dancing master and when he had taught her all he knew she went to Spain for six months to absorb the atmosphere, learn the language and acquire a new persona.

When she stepped on to the stage at Her Majesty's Theatre in London, she was Lola Montez. She was not a very good dancer. She had little sense of rhythm and timing. But, dressed in black lace and red roses she looked stunning and the management relied on her looks to bring in the crowds. But her first and only appearance on the London stage was a total disaster. To start with she was recognized by some young blade who called out 'Why, it's Betty James.' Then her exotic and highly provocative Tarantula dance, in which she conducted a frenzied search of her body for a lost spider, had to be brought to a swift end as the whole house erupted in hisses and catcalls.

Her mother, hearing of the shocking display her daughter was making of herself, decided that from that moment she no longer existed. She went into mourning and had her stationery edged with black.

Lola Montez

For a few years Lola drifted about Europe taking engagements where she could. To make herself interesting she swore at one point she had been reduced to singing in the streets of Brussels to keep herself from starving. She also told a fanciful tale about being engaged as a spy by the Tzar of Russia. She certainly *almost* met the Tzar. He was the guest of Frederick of Prussia at a Grand Fête where Lola had been engaged to dance. The following day a military tattoo was held in his honour. As the grand parade ended there was a sudden commotion among the onlookers. Lola appeared on horseback. Suddenly her mount, excited by the glitter and the noise – or perhaps by a sharp jab of spurs – headed straight for the royal box. Lola was on the point of being thrown into the Tzar's lap when a guard dashed forward and caught the reins. She rewarded him by raising her riding whip and bringing it down across his face.

Lola also gave a highly coloured version of her visit to Warsaw where her name first became involved in politics. She had been engaged to dance there and the Viceroy of Poland, a very rich old man, fell desperately in love with her. According to Lola he offered her a splendid country estate and handfuls of diamonds if she would become his mistress. He was, apparently, such a short, grotesque looking man that she respectfully declined.

The Viceroy was deeply insulted by the refusal. Next day the director of the theatre where she was appearing called on her and urged her to to reconsider the offer. He started by being persuasive then, seeing that he was getting nowhwere, threatened her. Fiery little Lola threw him out.

That night when she appeared on stage she was hissed and booed by a claque stationed in the gallery. It had obviously been arranged. The third night it happened Lola stamped up to the footlights in a rage, told the rest of the audience why she was being harassed and to her delight was overwhelmed by cheering and applause.

An immense crowd escorted her back to the hotel where she was staying. What she did not know was that both the Viceroy and the theatre manager were suspected of being traitors and the hatred the Polish people felt for their Tzarist-dominated government and its agents had suddenly found an outlet. The crowds did not go home. Rioting started in the streets and within 24 hours Warsaw was on the brink of revolution.

Told that her arrest had been ordered, she barricaded herself in her hotel room and informed the police when they arrived that she had a gun and would use it. The French Consul gallantly came forward and offered her his protection until the city quietened down. She was then asked to leave.

People were beginning to talk about Lola but not, she felt, quite enough. While in Dresden she met the Hungarian composer and pianist, Franz Liszt, who had half the women in Europe swooning over his profile and his demonic playing. She gazed into his eyes, and he was trapped. For a while they enjoyed a consuming passion, travelling everywhere together, quarrelling and making up interminably. They were a magnetic pair. But Liszt was a showman as well as a musician and it gradually dawned on him that Lola was stealing his thunder. His fears became certainty after a solemn occasion in Bonn at which he unveiled a statue to Beethoven. Lola, who had not been invited, gatecrashed the banquet that followed and before royalty and heads of state leaped on to a table and danced among the dishes.

After this Liszt realised he must get rid of her. One morning, while she was still asleep, he gathered his belongings together and crept out of their apartment, making sure to lock the door behind him. Passers-by were later astonished at the sight of furniture being thrown through a window by an enraged and beautiful woman.

She flounced off to Paris where her growing notoriety helped her to get an engagement at the Port Saint Martin Theatre. But nothing could cover the fact that her dancing was still second rate and that she couldn't pick up her feet in time to the music. She was hissed and this time answered her critics with a firework display of temper and a gesture for which she became famous. She took off her garters and flung them into the audience.

One night, intrigued by the stories he had heard about her, Henri Dujarier, literary critic and part owner of *La Presse*, went to see her dance. They were introduced backstage after her performance and found each other fascinating. Lola became his mistress and he began to show her a world she had never entered before. He took her to the salon of Georges Sand, Chopin's mistress. She met literary giants like Dumas, Victor Hugo, Balzac, and Gautier. She amazed them by her intelligence and, always interested in politics, she became an ardent republican like Dujarier. He asked her to marry him. But the idyll was not to last.

At a party one night Dujarier became involved in an argument with Jean de Beauvallon of *Le Globe*, a rival newspaperman he cordially disliked. The party ended with de Beauvallon challenging Dujarier to a duel. Lola was distraught. She knew her lover had never handled a duelling pistol in his life. De Beauvallon was a crack shot. She tried to persuade him not to take part but the duel took place at dawn and Dujarier was shot through the heart.

Lola grieved deeply and was the focus of all eyes at the sensational murder trial that followed. Swathed in black silk and lace she cried out: 'I could handle a pistol more accurately than poor Dujarier. I would have been quite willing to have gone out with M. de Beauvallon myself!'

But it was too late. The tragedy left her at the age of 27 quite comfortably off but in an emotional vacuum. There was nothing to do but go on dancing. She made up her mind to arrange a tour of Bavaria. It was the most important decision of her life and led to her greatest love affair, with King Ludwig I of Bavaria.

For King Ludwig nothing in the world mattered as much as art, sculpture, architecture and beauty. He lived in a cloud cuckoo land of Greek columns and classical verse, showing complete indifference to the ordinary, everyday needs of his country. He created modern Munich and made it the art centre of Germany but allowed his government to be dominated by reactionary elements and Jesuit priests.

He collected beautiful women in much the same way as he collected fine statues and it is highly likely that Lola, knowing his weakness, planned to take advantage of it. When she reached Munich the manager of the state theatre, after seeing her dance, explained ruefully that she was not good enough and took her name off the bill. Lola exploded and said she would appeal to Ludwig himself for help.

Having been kept waiting in Ludwig's ante-room for rather a long time she became impatient and decided to enter the royal presence without introduction. Just as she opened the door to Ludwig's private apartment a guard rushed forward to grab her and in the struggle tore the bodice of her dress. Lola swished through the door, slammed it behind her and was left facing an astounded Ludwig. His eyes became fixed on the torn bodice. Capriciously she snatched a pair of scissors from his desk and slashed it to the waist exposing her splendid bosom. Ludwig dismissed his *aide de camp* and before she left the palace she had been promised an engagement at the Munich Theatre.

The King went to see her dance three nights in succession and became completely infatuated. Five days later he presented her at court and astounded his ministers by introducing her as 'my best friend'.

At first not a voice was raised against her. Ludwig's Queen was used to his infidelities and did not realize that Lola was different from the rest. But it soon became clear that 'the Spanish dancer' was more than a mistress. She had political ambitions. Her first aim was to show the King how, while he had been busy collecting Greek statues and reading classic verse his government had become riddled with corruption and Jesuits had infiltrated everywhere. Within weeks she had exposed his Jesuit prime minister as a villain. She wanted above all to steer him towards republicanism and the whole country watched, appalled, as he hung on her every word. The Jesuits called her an 'emissary of Satan' and an 'Apocalyptic whore' and tried hard to 'bring the King to his senses'. But the minority Protestants in Bavaria regarded her as a heroine and a champion of liberty.

The relationship between Lola and Ludwig was complex. He undoubtedly loved her. He built her a small palace then, feeling it was not grand enough, added two wings of white marble, gilded and lavishly decorated, one of which housed an amazing glass staircase. He designed a marble fountain for the courtyard which sprayed delicately perfumed water. Lola felt she could not live in such splendour without a title so he created her Countess of Landsfeld and Baroness Rosenthal and gave her a gold trimmed coach lined with ermine to drive about in. People were beginning to say: 'What Lola wants, Lola gets.'

Her temper was as fiery as ever. She had thrown priceless vases at her interior decorators; the chief of police had had his ears boxed and she had thrown champagne at Ludwig's ministers during a state banquet. She became obsessed with a hatred of Jesuits and complained that they followed her everywhere. She bought a bulldog and taught it to snarl at the black-robed priests, even to bite them if necessary. She carried a whip and people learned to keep out of the way.

Realizing her influence over the King, even the most powerful ministers tried to win her favour. But the matter of her titles brought their real feelings into the open. Most ministers said she could not be ennobled unless she was naturalized – and they would never consent to naturalization. Ludwig, furious, not only raised her to Countess but also granted her an allowance from the treasury. The ruling ministry resigned and a new one was formed from advanced liberals. It became known as the 'Lola Ministry'. The bitter politicians said they had been driven from power by 'a strolling dancer of ill fame'.

Although she was young and full of idealistic fervour, she did not carry the students with her. And, to her cost, she did not realize soon enough the importance of student opinion.

One unpleasant incident brought about by this mistake contributed to her downfall. While she was out walking one day she ran into a Jesuit professor whom she hated because she suspected him of criticising her at the university. She set her bulldog on him. The deeply offended professor called a meeting of his colleagues to denounce Lola and her influence. Ludwig was told of the meeting and dismissed him. When they heard what had happened crowds of students gathered outside her palace shouting insults. She appeared defiantly on a balcony and stood there mockingly nibbling marzipan and sipping champagne. When she lifted her glass in a mock toast bricks began to fly through her window. The King, on being told what was happening, rushed to join her. For the first time in his life, he had to be provided with a military escort.

After this incident about 20 students who still supported her ideas rallied to her, forming a guard which became known as the *Alemannia*. They became very unpopular with their fellow students and soon the press was full of stories and lampoons about the Countess of Landsfeld and her male harem.

In the streets riots continued spasmodically, Lola's windows were protected with iron bars and everywhere she went she had to be escorted by members of the *Alemannia*, as showers of abuse and insult were hurled at her. Students frequently confronted her in the streets. On one of these occasions, flexing the whip she always carried she said in an icy voice: 'I will close down the university'. Nothing could have been worse.

Friends, advisers and members of his own family were by this time appealing to the distraught Ludwig to get rid of her. But he still loved her and he was stubborn. On 8 February 1848, to satisfy Lola he gave the order for the university to be closed. Hundreds rioted. Lola, by now feeling that nothing was beyond her, went out into the streets certain she could quell the violence, but as soon as she was recognised she was jostled and jeered. She tried to seek refuge at the Austrian Legation but no one would open the door for her. Eventually it was necessary to send for a detachment of soldiers to make sure she got back to her palace alive.

The King at last seemed to wake from his dream and realize that revolution was in the air. He was persuaded to take up a pen and with a shaking hand signed a document banishing Lola Montez from Bavaria. The mob was heading for her palace as she escaped through the back entrance and took to her carriage. Ludwig went to face the mob with great courage. Hatless, the strain showing on his face, he shouted 'Scoundrels. The house is empty. She is gone.' At least, he thought she had. But Lola couldn't quite accept what had happened to her and kept turning up in disguise, for one last farewell. Ludwig was asked to abdicate in favour of his son.

The rest of his life was devoted to a harmless study of architecture, painting and beautiful things, but he wrote long letters to the mistress who had cost him his crown and supported her with a pension for many years to come.

She arrived in London looking stunning in black velvet with a red rose in her hair. All the young women copied her and the fashionable young men tried to get to her parties so that they could say that they had met Lola Montez. One of these young blades was a Lifeguards officer called George Heald who was twenty years younger than her and due one day to inherit a fortune. She agreed to marry him only to find herself confronted with an army of aged relatives who had no intention of their money going to keep an adventuress. One of them, a rigid spinster who had brought up George, took time to dig into Lola's past and came up with her husband, Captain James, and the fact that since they parted in India they had never been legally divorced. Lola found herself on a bigamy charge at Marlborough Street Court. The besotted George stood bail for her and when nobody was looking they quietly left the country.

They managed to stay together for about three years but Lola's temper was getting worse and one day, after a terrible row, she stabbed him. He left her but, as he had done many times before, returned because he couldn't live without her. They were seen together in Spain at the Casino in Perpignan. Lola, wearing a flaming red gown, rubies flashing on her fingers, was the centre of attention. George Heald stood behind her chair. She kept putting her hand over her shoulder for more gold pieces. He ran out of funds. Next time the croupier called 'Faites vos jeux' she turned to her lover impatiently: 'Come, money, quick, money.' Flushing he replied 'you have played enough, come away. I have no more money.' Lola rose and struck him across the face. 'Learn,' she hissed 'that he who accompanies Lola must always have money at his command.'

She left him and their two children, and he began to drink his life away. Paris was her next hunting ground. Her income had dwindled so she appealed to Ludwig for funds which he provided and she was soon to be seen at the Café Royale looking exquisite in white silk and camellias and escorted by Prince Jung Bahadoor, the handsome Nepalese Ambassador.

But Europe was finished for Lola. She was looking for a new life and decided that the Americans would appreciate a dancer who was also a real life Countess. Barnum, the great showman, made her an offer, but she did not see herself as 'Lola, the Notorious Montez' exhibited along with his freaks. Instead she signed with an American agent called Edward Willis who considered her a lady and felt sure she could conquer the New World.

Lola made a spectacular arrival in New York in 1852 dressed in perfect gents' suiting with spurred, polished boots and a riding whip. One over-familiar American who dared to grab hold of her coat tails received a cut across the face for his pains.

Her progress across America was accompanied all the way by stories of her violent temper. She would rage at her critics and sometimes lash out with the whip so that managers began to ask themselves if she was worth the money. On reaching San Fransisco she found herself without an agent. He had just been told that back in New Orleans she had kicked the prompter and he had kicked her back; worn out with trying to smooth her path after such episodes, he handed in his notice.

While in California, she met and married a newspaperman called Patrick Hull, who reminded her of her old love Dujarier, and they set off on a tour of the gold rush towns, Lola taking with her 50 trunks containing silk draperies, gilt mirrors and exquisite *objets d'arts* as well as a stupendous wardrobe.

Her spider dance had become vulgar beyond words and it was said the miners would leave gold in the ground to see her perform it.

Patrick Hull lasted only a few weeks. Though charming he turned out to have an Irish will as fierce as her own. One night she threw his belongings out of the window and he went back to his newspaper.

When she wasn't touring she lived in a white painted house in Grass Valley and came near to settling there for good. She loved the scenery and became devoted to her menagerie of animals, including a grizzly bear which she took for walks. But her huge expenditure on entertaining, even when she was supposed to be living simply, made it neccessary for her to keep on dancing.

She became attracted to a small time theatrical manager called Ned Fellin, who obviously saw Lola as a means of making his name. He suggested a world tour in 1855 to include Australia, Paris and New York. They became lovers and set out to storm the antipodes.

Lola shocked Australia. After what she considered a tasteful version of 'Tarantula' in Sydney she was found to be 'suggestive' and 'indelicate'. She moved on to Melbourne where a local editor called her performance 'immoral'. She went after him armed with a whip. At Geelong the audience called upon the mayor to stop her act and at Ballarat, where at least the miners cheered her, she attacked the editor of the local paper, only to be given a taste of her own medicine. Eventually they had to admit that the Australian tour was a failure and they agreed to go home to America.

Fellin had become tiresome as far as Lola was concerned – far too sensitive about her little flirtations. Afterwards Lola said little of the mysterious incident that ended their relationship, but it was obviously traumatic.

On the night of 18 July 1856 they were on board ship, heading for home. They had reached Fiji and Fellin apparently asked Lola for some money she had in reserve. She went to her cabin to fetch it. Suddenly there was a terrible scream. People rushed on deck to find Lola lying in a dead faint. Fellin was nowhere to be seen. A thorough search was made but to no avail. He had simply disappeared. When questioned about precisely what happened that night Lola would never discuss details but would say 'I have been wild and wayward, but never wicked' implying that Fellin had not met his death at her hands, but had fallen overboard.

Back in America she was a different woman. Her temper seemed under control, she never again carried a whip and she turned to religion. She disappeared at the end of 1856 and did not appear on the scene again for a year. It was rumoured she had married again, though when asked the name of her husband she would laugh and dismiss the matter. Years later in the records of the royal family of Bavaria was found a record of a morganatic marriage between Lola Montez and Ludwig. He was then 72. If so then means must have been found to dissolve her marriage with Captain James.

By 1859 she was thinner, her hair came out in handfuls and her dress became slovenly. She was desperately ill and she knew it. She sought consolation more and more in religion and spiritualism, boarding at a Methodist hotel where she rented two furnished, pleasant rooms. After suffering a slight stroke she was taken under the wing of a so-called fervent Christian called Mrs Buchanan, who persuaded her to go and live with her and her husband.

News of Lola's illness reached her mother, now Lady Craigie, and the avaricious woman travelled to America on the pretext of seeing her daughter for the last time, but in fact to ascertain whether Lola still had Ludwig's jewels. What she did not know was that the cunning Mrs Buchanan had persuaded the sick woman to hand over the few pieces she had left, including a diamond necklace, with the promise that she would look after her till the end.

Disappointed, Lady Craigie went home leaving 10 dollars towards the care of her dying daughter. The evil Mrs Buchanan moved Lola to a wretched hovel of a boarding house and left her there in the care of a filthy old hag.

The Protestant Minister who visited her at the end thought naively that she had chosen this place as a penitence for all the bad years. He stayed with her and gave her comfort as she died like a pauper on a pile of rags.

Barbara Villiers

There came a point in the reign of Charles II when people began to wonder who really ruled England; the amiable, amoral King or his mistress, Barbara Villiers. Her power over him was absolute, her avarice insatiable and her temper formidable.

Through the corrupt practices of the beautiful Barbara, the whole administration was tainted. Lord Clarendon, the great Chancellor she brought to ruin, could not bring himself to utter her name – he always called her 'That Lady' – and diarist, John Evelyn, fuming about her morals, called her 'the curse of our nation'.

Her greed was never satisfied. When Charles had given her all he could she plundered public funds for money to buy houses and jewels. She dominated the Keeper of the Privy Purse to such an extent that he gave her thousands of pounds that should have been spent on the royal household. Soon it became known that the only way to advance a career in government or at court was

Charles II

to apply to the King's mistress for a place or preferment – and to pay her accordingly. The King would eventually agree to anything to avoid Barbara's wrath.

No one is quite certain how they met. It was probably just before his return from exile when she and her husband, as true Royalists, went to the Continent to offer him their support on regaining the throne. She was then at the height of her beauty, tall, with a glorious figure, midnight black hair and flashing, imperious blue eyes. She became his mistress and his obsession. Her great hold on him, it was believed, was her incredible sexual prowess, for the King was a very sensual man.

On the momentous day when Charles returned from exile to a tumultuous welcome in the city of London and retired to what contemporary historians called: 'his sweet and sedate repose'; it was Barbara Villiers, in all her glory, who waited to greet him in the royal bed.

The Villiers family, from which she sprang, had produced some of the most successful and powerful courtiers since the time of the Norman Conquest. They had a long history of intimacy with Kings. Barbara was born in 1641 in the parish of St Margaret's, Westminster. Her father, William Villiers, Viscount Grandison, fought for the Royalists at the Battle of Edgehill and died of his wounds at the seige of Bristol when she was only three. Her mother then married a cousin, Charles Villiers, a decent but relatively poor man, and Barbara was brought up in the country without luxury.

Taken to London at the age of 16 she soon showed her true metal and became involved with one of the most notorious rakes in town, the 23-year-old Earl of Chesterfield, who admitted he would sleep with any woman provided she was not old or ugly. He had the upper hand where Barbara was concerned and she suffered agonies of jealousy. The experience made her vow that in future affairs she would be dominant.

When she was 18 she married Roger Palmer, son of a wealthy and respected country knight who was studying law. Scholarly and quiet he hardly seemed the partner for Barbara Villiers. But, having fallen in love with her, nothing would do but marriage and her own family encouraged the match.

Their wedding took place on 14 April 1659 and the minute it was over Roger whisked his bride away to the country. He hoped to be able to keep her from temptation, but his efforts were futile. Half crazy with boredom, she wrote passionate letters to Chesterfield and slipped away to see him whenever she could. The affair ended when the Earl killed a man in a duel, fled to the Continent and, to her fury, married someone else.

But if Palmer thought his worries were over with Chesterfield's departure, he had no idea of what was to come. Once his wife had met the King, Palmer ceased to exist as far as she was concerned – except to play the role of father to her offspring.

He seems to have had no idea what was going on at first, but when he suddenly gained the title Earl of Castlemaine shortly after the birth of Barbara's first royal child he had to face the truth. Public sympathy was very much for Roger Palmer who had served the Stuarts well and sufffered great injustice. Although he lived to a great age he never took his seat in the House of Lords and hardly ever used his title.

There was no doubt that the King's mistress was the most dazzling figure at Court. By 1662 her power over the monarch was growing daily. He dined with her nearly every night, hardly ever appeared in public without her and was plainly influenced by her opinions. Her very presence at Court seemed to create an atmosphere of tension and unease. Her manner was so imperious and arrogant that many of the great nobles became hostile towards her. Lord Clarendon was particularly aware of the danger in her growing influence and did everything he could to curb it. Nor did it go unnoticed that her Ladyship now dressed in clothes and jewels of great splendour and extravagance.

Just as she was at her zenith, Barbara was brought down to earth with a shock. The King told her he was to be married and implied that her position would be somewhat changed by the arrival of his bride. 'The whole affair,' Samuel Pepys noted gleefully in his diary 'will put Madame Castlemaine's nose out of Joynt.'

Charles travelled to Portsmouth to meet the ship bringing Catherine of Braganza, Infanta of Portugal, to be his Queen. Himself gloriously tailored in velvet and lace, he was somewhat surprised by the frumpy appearance of his bride and her equally dowdy ladies-in-waiting. Short, plain, swarthy-complexioned, the Portuguese princess was nothing like the women Charles found attractive. But it was a political marriage and the King had enough good in him to recognize her qualities. He found her sweet and pious and her conversation proved most agreeable.

While the royal pair made a magnificent progress to Hampton Court, Barbara, eight months pregnant, was impatiently kicking her heels. She was eventually delivered of a son. Her husband, a recent convert to Rome, had the boy baptised by a priest. He was only playing the part expected of him, but when his wife heard the news she exploded with rage, packed her bags and went to live in her brother's house in Richmond, swearing that she would never again live with Lord Castlemaine. Her reaction was calculated. In one stroke she had managed to rid herself of her husband and move nearer to the King.

For a short time after the arrival of Catherine, Lady Castlemaine stayed out of sight. But then Charles himself precipitated a scene which profoundly shocked the Court. He was horrified by the unattractive, prudish women his Queen had brought with her as ladies-in-waiting. He thought it time to appoint a few English beauties to the Queen's bedchamber in the hope that his wife would be influenced by their taste and refinement. Barbara begged and pleaded with him to allow her to be one of them as a public demonstration of his loyalty to her.

When the Queen saw Lady Castlemaine's name at the top of the list Charles presented to her, she fainted with shock. She refused even to set eyes on the woman of whom she had heard so much. Her mother had told her never to allow her name to be mentioned in her presence. The King

Barbara Villiers

withdrew, murmuring apologies but Barbara pestered him so much that he decided to try once more. This time he led her into the Queen's presence without warning and asked to be allowed to present her. Catherine, face to face with the dreaded mistress fell down in a fit, blood pouring from her nose, and the Court scattered in confusion.

Clarendon, who had supported the Queen all along was called to issue an ultimatum. Either Catherine accepted Lady Castlemaine or the King would feel free to have as many mistresses as he chose. The Queen gave in for, though she had been cruelly humiliated, she had grown to love Charles. In fact the row marked a turning point in their relationship. The King discovered he had grown fond of his plain little wife, although he had a poor way of showing it.

Her success over the business of the bedchamber made Barbara even more demanding and arrogant. She travelled in the royal coach with the King and even persuaded him to break his solemn promise to Catherine not to allow her to live under the royal roof. She was given an apartment next to the King so they could live together almost as man and wife. At this point her influence over him was quite sinister. She knew his weaknesses better than anyone and enslaved him with her passion, often when he should have been attending to affairs of state.

Meddling in politics was one of her worst faults. She had no particular allegiance but just wanted to get rid of those who opposed her or who objected to the fortune she made out of selling important posts. She talked Charles into getting rid of many of his elder statesmen so that she could replace them with her own favourites. Lord Clarendon, whom she still hated and feared once remarked bitterly: 'That woman would sell every place if she could.' The words were reported to her and she replied tartly that his Lordship could rest easy for his place was already contracted for and the bargain near completion!

Money was her God. She raided the privy purse to pay her ever increasing debts and squandered thousands of pounds in gambling or in reckless spending. The King dared not cross her. Sometimes when she was displeased, she would summon him from some important meeting and berate him like a fishwife.

The first sign of a crack in her Ladyship's power came with the arrival from France of a new lady-in-waiting for the Queen. Although she was only 15 and a distant relation, the King was captivated the moment he set eyes on her. Her name was Frances Stuart though her porcelain prettiness had earned her the title La Belle Stuart. She was the opposite of the King's voluptuous mistress in every way. Fresh and sweet natured, she knew how to flirt deliciously while keeping him at arm's length. She had no interest in politics or intrigue. Barbara watched her rival flitting about the Court like some exquisite butterfly and treated everyone to bouts of her foul temper. The fact that she was heavily pregnant with yet another of the King's children and needed to rest, made his dalliance all the easier. But though the ardent Charles wooed Frances Stuart with all the charm he possessed, he did not win her. She was in love with the young Duke of Richmond and one night eloped with him. The Court was startled by the King's jealous anger and not too happy to see Lady Castlemaine back again, all powerful.

With Frances Stuart out of the way, the King's mistress now turned her venom on her old enemy, Clarendon.

Politically and economically England had been through a difficult time both at home and abroad. Lord Clarendon, as the King's chief minister and one of the few experienced politicians left, was blamed for a good deal of it. Talk against him was inflamed by Barbara and her associates until in the end even Charles, who owed him so much, felt he must go. What really irritated the King was his Chancellor's puritanical attitude and obvious distate for the libertine Court. In the interview that took place between them, Clarendon was unwise enough to speak out against Lady Castlemaine and her meddling in state affairs. The King was furious and told him to hand in his seal of office and never return. As Clarendon left, devastated, the King's mistress was seen on a balcony in her nightclothes laughing and jeering him on his way.

The fall of Clarendon convinced Barbara that she could do anything with the King. He was clay in her hands. Once she forced him to beg her forgiveness on his knees while the court looked on appalled at his weakness and her power.

During their affair neither had been faithful to the other. So profligate was the court of Charles II that infidelity was regarded as a trifle. Barbara became infatuated with a world-famous rope dancer, a handsome fellow called Jacob Hall, and it was said she gave him a pension from money intended for national defence. Another lover was a back-stairs page, who later became an actor. Then there was a young footman who accompanied her coach and whom, malicious tongues said, was forced to take a bath with her.

When she became pregnant for the sixth time, Charles knew the child was not his. When he accused her of infidelity and suggested the notorious rake, Henry Jermyn, was more likely to be the father, she threatened to publish his letters if he did not accept paternity. For once Charles stood firm. In a dreadful scene she swore that if he did not acknowledge the child she would bring it to court and dash out its brains in front of everybody. 'God damn you! But you *shall* own it!' she screeched. She had gone too far.

His wisest councillors began to advise the King to dismiss Barbara – and he listened to them. It was time for a change. He took Moll Davies, a common actress, as his mistress and set her up in a splendid house in Suffolk Street. But she was soon eclipsed by another who was to delight Charles for the rest of his life. Her name was Nell Gwynne and she was a match for Lady Castlemaine as well as a salve for Charles's battered ego.

Though their days as lovers were over, Barbara now began to take advantage of her new status. For it was while Charles was making the effort to rid himself of her that she cost him most. To keep her quiet he bestowed yet more titles upon her so that in 1670 she became Duchess of Cleveland, Countess Nonsuch and Countess of Southampton. These favours of course meant yet more money from the privy purse so that she could live the life of a Duchess. People thought that with the bestowal of the title and the lands that went with it she would be satisfied. They did not know she was also receiving £30,000 a year, money to settle her debts and enormous sums from the Customs and Excise and Post Office revenues.

Although her affair with the King had virtually come to an end she still had enough beauty at the age of 30 to raise men's blood pressure when she chose. The great Duke of Marlborough, then a handsome young man of 21 newly arrived from Devon, became her lover and she bore his child. The King was said not to mind in the least but he wished, if she was having an affair 'not to make such a damned show of it'. Her influence at court was now entirely eclipsed by the King's latest favourite, a beautiful Breton girl called Louise de Keroualle.

Charles dipped into public funds once more in 1674 for lavish weddings for two of Barbara's daughters, Charlotte, who became Countess of Litchfield and Anne, who became Countess of Sussex. But this time people came out into the streets and demonstrated against this latest extravagance of 'the King's whore'.

Two years later Barbara Villiers, new Duchess of Cleveland, took herself off to Paris where she took as many lovers as she pleased and managed to bring about the downfall of the British Ambassador.

Throughout her life abroad she and the King exchanged letters and when she returned to London in 1685 the diarist, John Evelyn, recorded that she was graciously received by him. She was certainly one of a group playing cards with the King a few nights before he had the seizure which brought about his death.

Years passed and the days when she dominated the Court with her arrogance and beauty must have seemed a long way off. Her gambling debts were huge and the money she had accumulated had slipped away, largely falling into the hands of rogues.

In 1705, when she was 64, she allowed herself to be talked into marriage with a reprobate called Beau Fielding who had been married twice and had already squandered two fortunes. The match was the talk of the season and the subject of some cruel satires. Fielding, discovering that the Duchess of Cleveland was not as wealthy as he had supposed, beat her so violently that she thought she would die. Fortunately evidence was produced to show that the rogue had never been divorced from his first wife and he was marched off to court for bigamy.

After the shame of this episode she spent her last years in her house in Chiswick Mall near the Thames, known today as Walpole House. Her once glorious body swelled with dropsy and she died there on 9 October 1709. But her spirit, always restless and unsatisfied in life, would not rest and she is said to haunt the Mall to this day.

Eliza Lynch

By the muddy bank of the river Aquidaban in Paraguay, only a stone's throw from the Bolivian border, a beautiful Irish woman knelt to dig a grave with her bare hands. She had asked to be allowed to bury the body of her lover, and the son who died with him, at the end of what was one of the bloodiest and most futile wars ever fought in South America.

The horror of the scene was one she could not have envisaged in all the years through which she, and the man whose corpse she now covered with stones, had dreamed and schemed to make Paraguay a dominant power and themselves, Emperor and Empress of the South American states.

The woman's name was Eliza Lynch who for 16 years had been the mistress of Francisco Solano López; a vain, ruthless megalomaniac who succeeded his father as President of Paraguay. Together they had precipitated a war against the combined forces of Brazil, Argentina and Uruguay which ended with cities in ruins, the economy destroyed and half the population dead.

They first came together in a totally different world.

In the year 1854 Eliza Alicia Lynch from County Cork had never even heard of Paraguay. She was just another pretty courtesan who had set herself up in Paris hoping to make her fortune. Her family had fled from Ireland in the great famine with hopes of making a new life in France. Eliza was married at 15 to a French officer, Xavier Quatrefages, but as being his wife condemned her to live in a hot, dusty Algerian outpost, she soon thought better of it. By 18 she was back in Paris and ready for a different kind of life.

She became a courtesan because she could think of no other way for a girl like her to live in wealth and luxury. Through a few fortunate introductions she got herself into the élite circle around Princess Mathilde and soon she was seen at every great occasion.

Her Junoesque figure, golden hair and provocative smile attracted men by the dozen, but she didn't want a dozen. She wanted only one who was prepared to commit himself and his money to a long liaison and become not only her lover but her protector. The French had proved too fickle so she decided it must be a foreigner. She told her servants to leave her card at the best hotels and foreign embassies. On it she had printed 'Madame Lynch, Instructress in languages'. She obviously preferred to forget her husband Quatrefages.

Before long it became the fashionable thing to call on Madame Lynch, exchange a few words (she spoke Spanish and French as well as English) and play a few cards. One day, staring across the room at her, she saw an ugly little man with a pear-shaped head, a negroid nose and a mouthful of dark brown teeth, the front ones missing. His teeth were clenched on a huge cigar. 'Who on earth is that?' she asked someone. Told that it was Francisco López, the immensely rich eldest son of the dictator-president of Paraguay, she became very interested.

By the following morning they were lovers and López, totally infatuated, asked Eliza to return with him to South America. She had listened to his egotistical talk and to his grandiose plans for becoming Emperor. She realized that if she linked her destiny to his she would have to encourage him in his mad ambitions, continually reassure him that he was a fascinating man and turn a blind eye to his coarse nature. She did not even know where Paraguay was but he made it sound like an earthly paradise. Her answer was yes.

They went off on a European honeymoon, López buying his new mistress all the diamonds, furs and beautiful gowns she wanted. On visiting Napoleon's tomb he made note that he would order one exactly the same for himself. But his ageing father had been bombarding him with pleas to come home and on the morning of 11 November 1854 they sailed.

Eliza took with her a vast wardrobe of Paris gowns, trunks full of household linen, an elaborate table service and cases and cases of Sèvres porcelain as well as opulent furniture and a Pleyel piano. López took a large number of ornate uniforms. She had a vision of herself bringing European culture, refinement and style to the Paraguayans and felt sure they would love her. If she had a model in mind, it was probably the Empress Eugenie.

Her reception was not quite what she expected. The 1,000 mile journey up river to the capital, Asunción, was made in terrible heat and humidity. It was a colourful world she looked out on – floating islands of water lilies, crocodiles and orange trees – but she was pregnant and felt sick. The 'First Family' was waiting to greet them on the quay, lined up in their separate carriages.

The President himself, Carlos Antonio, answered her smile with a few grunts. The López women – Francisco's mother and two sisters – frumpily dressed in black – stared with hostility at the figure in pale lilac silk and drove off without a word. She did not know that while his family had no objection to him womanising at home, they would not tolerate a foreigner. She was known before she arrived as 'the Irish strumpet' and the women had tried hard to get the old President to forbid her entry.

Eliza was appalled by the sight of Francisco's 'paradise' for when the dust settled Asunción showed itself to be a dilapidated and dismal place. She decided there and then that it must be rebuilt, whatever the cost.

Francisco did his best to get his family to accept Eliza, without success. But here, on his home ground she began to learn what he was really like. His only real interest, apart from women, was in power for himself and war. He considered himself a military genius like Napoleon. He was a cruel profligate who considered any virgin to be fair game. Many of the noblest families in Paraguay sent their daughters abroad rather than risk having them raped by López. One girl threatened that she would commit suicide if he touched her and another, about to marry, was presented with her bridegroom's body as a wedding present after refusing to submit.

Eliza knew all this. She knew about his visits to brothels, too. She decided to accept his appetites but told him that if he was going to have concubines she would choose them for him. She had already given birth to his son and he built her a pink and white palace, a *quinta*, the first two-storied habitation in Paraguay. She was to have six more children before she was 32.

The old aristocratic families treated her as a whore and their womenfolk averted their eyes as she passed. Many of the foreign wives also went out of their way to snub her. She put up with it for seven years, shrugging her white shoulders and concealing her bitterness with smiles. Then came the moment she had been waiting for. The old President died. Francisco told her she was now First Lady of Paraguay. He made it clear to everyone that his mistress was to be accorded the courtesy and honour due to any consort. She was ready to play the part to the hilt. When the time was ripe she would repay ruthlessly those who had insulted her.

Within a month of his succession, López had imprisoned or exiled more than 1,000 prominent men whose loyalty he suspected. Those who left quietly through the back door had made a shrewd assessment of the new President and his lady and smelt danger.

The old dictator's dying words to his son had been to settle troubles with the pen rather than the sword. He had come to realize that his son was of such an explosive nature that leaving him in command of the powerful military force he had built up in Paraguay was like leaving a lunatic in a fireworks factory.

But Eliza encouraged him in his vanity and illusions of military grandeur. She had come into her own. Anyone who failed in paying due respect was humiliated. The newly appointed British Minister was rash enough to say he had no intention of recognizing the 'Paraguayan Pompadour'. She suggested to López that he should be made to present his credentials walking the length of Asunción instead of arriving in state. The proud ladies of the capital soon got the message. They began to call on the First Lady in droves, full of sweet compliments only to tear her to bits when they were out of hearing.

Eliza then had her position threatened in a way she had never dreamed of. López, who swore to her he would never marry anyone else asked Dom Pedro of Brazil for his daughter's hand. It was a terrible shock to her. Alan Brodsky, who served with the US Embassy at Asunción in 1955 and has written a detailed account of the Lynch-López relationship explains 'The dream they shared – a not entirely unrealistic one, given the circumstances of the time – was to convert Paraguay into the capital of an empire that would embrace the entire Rio de la Plata region: Paraguay itself, the Argentine Confederation, Uruguay and Brazil. . . . . .' Of course, she saw herself as Empress of this great vision and never thought it would be otherwise.

But Eliza had nothing to worry about. The Emperor of Brazil considered López to be 'licentious, dissolute and cruel' and as Madame Lynch had such an influence over him, she was probably just the same. Nothing would induce him to give his daughter to such a man. By this reply Dom Pedro made himself a bitter enemy.

Somehow López had to make amends to Eliza, fuming in her pink and white *quinta*. He arranged for her to have enough funds to give a dazzling succession of balls, fêtes and suppers, showing the 'provincial' ladies of Asunción how it was done in Paris. But it was not enough. She wanted more say in the affairs of state and assumed the title of Minister without Portfolio.

She could sense something in the air. The whole continent was in a state of unrest, the two giants, Brazil and Argentina, beginning to rumble like unquiet volcanos and Uruguay, the small country between them fearing for her independence. She turned to Paraguay as an ally. Scenting trouble, López put his country on a war footing.

For the next few weeks all the South American countries engaged in brinkmanship that could only lead to disaster. López, after one successful diplomatic effort regarding Argentina, imagined himself as a go-between, but he only succeeded in making things worse. He continually sent bombastic notes to everybody, demanding to know what was going on. Thanks to his statesmanship, Uruguay and Brazil were soon at war with each other. His only contribution as the former's ally seems to have been a complaint that he was being ignored!

Behind it all Eliza schemed and conferred with the few men who were her close confidantes and admirers. She wanted war. She was convinced now that the only way Paraguay could gain consequence was by taking up arms against one of the major South American powers. Thornton, the British Minister, advised his superiors at the Foreign Office: 'Her orders, which are given imperiously, are obeyed as implicitly and with as much servility as those of the President himself.' In other words people were beginning to fear her.

When Brazil invaded Uruguay and became bogged down there, she urged López to invade Brazil. Still seething under the insult from Dom Pedro, who thought so little of him as a son-in-law, Francisco listened carefully. One day the largest steamer in the Brazilian merchant fleet was about to enter Paraguayan waters with a routine shipment of gold. It was seized and charged with a violation of national waters. Many of those on board, including the governor of Matto Grosso were sent to a prison in the Interior, never to be seen again. López now threw his soldiers into a war with Brazil that had never been declared. He took his troops up the Paraná river and the Brazilians, not prepared for invasion, fled leaving all their ammunition behind. Within fifteen days all the territory claimed by Paraguay had been occupied. López sent news of his triumph back to Asunción. Eliza, glorying in his success, staged a four-hour military parade on the Campo Grando, a huge plain outside the capital. She also gave a ball and other celebrations that went on and on and on.

But López, by his aggression and disregard for international law, had made everyone his enemy. As in some mad quadrille, everyone in South America changed partners. His three powerful neighbours, Brazil, Argentina and Uruguay, now joined against him in what was called the Treaty of the Triple Alliance. They were determined to crush him, though through bad leadership and ineptitude on all sides the war which ruined Paraguay was to drag on for five years.

Eliza had taken to collecting jewellery. She appealed to every woman to give up her treasured pieces to help López fight the war. That way she really got her claws into the aristocrats and the self-righteous ladies of Asunción who had snubbed her. She had memorised all the really fine pieces they owned. If they were not produced at the first asking, she asked again. She got her revenge. Most of the jewels were never seen again by their owners.

The war, bloody and terrible as it was, brought López to his knees. He lost half his army and most of his navy. It soon became obvious that only a miracle could save Paraguay from disaster. Eliza knew now she would never be Empress of anywhere. She had no intention of spending the rest of her life in a war battered Paraguay and was determined not to leave as a pauper. Already a consignment of jewels had been sent to her agent in Paris. More followed as she continued her collection for the brave López. She also managed through sheer bluff, to remove four cases of gold coins from the treasury, which she had loaded on to an Italian sailing ship heading for France.

Still, she did not abandon López. She moved up to the headquarters at Humaitá where the Brazilians were firing 4,000 shells a day, but so inaccurately that they caused little damage. She would order gourmet meals to be served to her with wine but López preferred plates of greasy food washed down with brandy. Sometimes when he was drunk, the calamity of his position would strike him and he would order executions. Full of frustration he would cry out that he would pardon nobody. Before the war was over he had tortured and killed without mercy everyone from the common soldier to members of his own family. His brother-in-law, Treasurer General Bedoya, was accused of stealing four cases of gold coins and subjected to such terrible torture that he died. Eliza said not a word.

Humaitá fell to the Brazilians on 25 July 1868 and soon most of the Paraguayan cities were in Allied hands. López gathered the remnants of his army together, along with his family and his mistress, and fled. In one final attempt at stopping the enemy reaching Asunción he threw everything he had into a pitched battle. In it, 5,000 Paraguayan troops died, most of them old men, young boys, cripples and women. López had lost or killed practically a whole generation.

The end came on 1 March 1870 when the Brazilians caught up with him and his wretched band of fugitives at his last 'capital' at Cerro Cora on the banks of the Rio Aquidaban. When he heard that the Brazilian cavalry, led by General Camarra, had broken through, he ordered his last few soldiers to make a human wall while he tried to make his escape on a horse. But the horse floundered in the mud and López was shot as he struggled to his knees. His final words were: 'I die with my country.'

His mother and two sisters, whom he had condemned to death only hours before as paranoia took him over, surrendered themselves. Eliza had made a dash to the carriage always kept waiting for her and attempted to escape with her youngest sons. But Camarra caught up with her and led her back to the place where López lay dead. She then buried him.

A Brazilian gunboat took the women back to Asunción. The López women returned to their homes but Eliza was kept on board for her own safety. Camarra was warned that if the women in Asunción had been able to get their hands on her they would have killed her. Refusing to hand her over to the provisional government, he put her on board ship for Europe. She had caused enough trouble.

Eliza Lynch was 35 when she got back to London. The most conservative estimate of the valuables she had managed to slip out of Paraguay was about one third of a million pounds, besides other investments she had been able to make. She lived in London for the rest of her life, presenting herself as the victim of a gross miscarriage of justice. She looked handsome and distinguished and was much admired.

Most of her time was spent over legal wrangles and trying to get what she considered belonged to her. For instance there was the matter of two small fortunes which she and López had given to a certain Dr William Stewart to send out of the country. They had gone astray. Some years later, she returned to Asunción, perhaps after Francisco's money which had been willed to her. Although she talked on her return of weeping women kissing her hand as she passed by there was a move to have her brought to trial.

She died on 27 July 1886. Her death certificate gave her respectability. It described her as 'The widow of Francisco S. López.' Time, too, had its softening effect on her reputation. On the 144th anniversary of Francisco López's birth the urn bearing her remains was carried in procession to her last resting place in Asunción. And the descendants of her liaison with the man who wanted to be an Emperor, had her proclaimed a national heroine.

Chapter Two

Scandalous Wives

Women who have proved monumental headaches
to their husbands range from the frankly lethal to
those who simply ignored the accepted code of
behaviour for the day and created scandals that
rocked their era. . . .

Violet Trefusis

On 16 June 1919 a society wedding took place at St George's, Hanover Square in London which caused many people to heave a sigh of relief. Looking exquisite in a gown of old *Valenciennes* lace, Violet Keppel became Mrs Denys Trefusis and that, they said, should settle the matter once and for all.

The handsome couple were waved off on their honeymoon, crossed the Channel and booked into the Ritz Hotel in Paris. But before the suitcases could be unpacked, Violet was scribbling tortured, passionate letters to her lover, letters crying: 'What am I now? A heartbroken nonentity, a lark with clipped wings. I feel so desperate...' Before the honeymoon was over, Violet Trefusis was in her lover's arms, leaving her husband to sob quietly in his room and it was quite obvious that the matter had not been settled at all.

It was just one more stage in an affair that people felt they could only refer to in shocked whispers. For the lover Violet Trefusis refused to let go when the wedding ring was slipped on her finger was Vita Sackville West, writer, poet, mother of two sons and wife of English diplomat, Harold Nicolson.

The two of them first met at a tea party when they were only children and discovered they both liked horses and read the same books. Both were the product of upper class homes with nannies and governesses and both had forceful, glamorous mothers.

Violet was the elder daughter of Mrs Alice Keppel, the famous Edwardian society hostess whose good looks, charm and discretion made her a favourite companion of King Edward VII. Her father was third son of the Earl of Albemarle. As an exceptionally pretty little girl she was doted on, spoiled and usually managed to get her own way. She resented discipline of any kind.

When she grew into a young woman she was sent off abroad so that she could aquire polish and learn to speak French, Italian and Spanish fluently. She always wanted to be the centre of attention and usually managed it with her vivacity, her husky voice and great grey eyes. She became a terrible flirt, throwing over first one man, then another, perhaps in an effort to compete with her dauntingly fascinating mother.

Denys Trefusis was 28 when she was introduced to him, an officer in the Royal Horse Guards with reddish gold hair and startling blue eyes. Highly intelligent, there was something different about him that attracted her. Then she discovered that though he had been brought up as an English public schoolboy and taught to love church, army and throne, he had run off to

Russia where he had earned a living teaching the children of an aristocractic family. He had learned to speak Russian fluently and there was something of the slav about him. He had come back to England to join up. Violet decided she was going to make him fall in love with her.

Trefusis spent a gallant war in the trenches and won the MC. Violet's warm, witty, clever letters had no doubt kept him going. She seduced him by post and when the poor, unsuspecting man proposed, she said 'yes'. But there was, of course, the problem of Vita.

When they met again as grown women, the attraction was mutual: Violet, vibrantly feminine, reckless and free, and Vita tall, languid, and with the elegance of a handsome boy. But Vita was happily married and adored the husband she called 'Hadji'.

Their 'scandalous' affair started when Violet was a guest at the Nicolson's beautiful country house in Kent in the April of 1918. She had asked if she might stay for a few days to get out of the London bombing. Vita was not too sure. She thought they might end up bored with each other. But Violet got her own way, as usual.

One night, Harold Nicolson did not return for dinner but stayed at his club in London for the night. That was when Violet with infinite subtlety and worldliness told Vita she loved her. Two kisses were exchanged. Vita did not sleep that night. Vita's son, Nigel Nicolson told the story of what followed in his *Portrait of a Marriage* in which he is absolutely frank about both his parents' inclinations in the sexual sphere.

After that traumatic night they went off for holidays together staying at Hugh Walpole's cottage at Polperro in Cornwall. Vita's mother, Lady Sackville, told everybody 'they have gone to see the Spring flowers,' thinking they had. One of Violet's letters, recalling that time says 'Sometimes we loved each other so much that we became inarticulate, content only to probe each other's eyes for the secret that was a secret no longer.'

That autumn Vita began to write *Challenge*, the book in which she and Violet are depicted as the lovers, Julian and Eve, and before long they began to act out the fantasy. Vita, dressed as a subaltern, would stroll through the streets of London with Violet on her arm and, as a laughing young couple they would join others enjoying a spot of leave at tea dances and restaurants. They took an enormous risk. Vita may have thought her disguise impenetrable, but Violet was such a well known society girl, they could easily have been caught out.

Denys Trefusis had appeared on the scene. He was desperately in love with Violet and did not look forward to having Harold Nicolson's wife as a rival. Violet made the almost impossible demand that if she married him she would not have to sleep with him and could continue her relationship with Vita.

Vita Sackville West

Thinking, no doubt, that things would work out in time, Trefusis agreed.

That same autumn the two women managed to get away to Monte Carlo for a short break. Amazingly Harold consented to get permits for them through his special influence at the Foreign Office as it was impossible to leave England without them at that time. As his son states, he could not have been ignorant of what was going on and even Lady Sackville was beginning to fear the worst.

Their little jaunt was supposed to last no more than a fortnight, but they stayed away for four months. When they reached Paris Violet tried to get Vita to stay with her for always, saying she would kill herself if Vita did not agree. These scenes were repeated every time Vita tried to book a passage home.

Violet thought of herself as a true rebel. She wanted to shock society and thought that by openly flaunting convention she would show that love had more dimensions than people dreamed of. However, Harold Nicolson did not see it that way, as he first spent a Christmas without his wife, then found by New Year that she had even stopped writing to him. For the first time he became really angry. Lady Sackville relieved her feelings by calling Violet 'that viper' and 'that pervert' and by writing to all her friends that her daughter had been bewitched.

At last they came home. Violet, largely to please her mother whom she adored, got engaged to Denys Trefusis on 2 March 1919. This did not stop her writing to Vita, telling her how much she ached for her and demanding 'Are you going to stand by and let me marry this man?'

She planned to elope with Vita the day before the wedding. They spent a lot of time together at Long Barn, the Nicolsons' home, and she nearly went mad with jealousy when Harold came home on leave.

'You and he, strolling about arm in arm (God I *shall* go mad!)' she wrote. 'I hate men. They fill me with revulsion. Even quite small boys.'

After the wedding and that travesty of a honeymoon Violet and Denys Trefusis came back to England to live at Possington Manor near Uckfield in Sussex. Violet was already talking of separation. She showed her husband all Vita's letters and he angrily burned them. The passionate correspondence started up again and soon they were back to the old routine, pretending to be Julian and Eve, slipping across to Paris and making everybody thoroughly miserable.

The crisis came in January 1920, when the two women decided to go away together for good — and this time they meant it. By now Denys Trefusis was talking incoherently about shooting somebody, which was not really surprising considering the strain he was under.

Practically everybody turned up on the quayside at Dover. Violet had gone ahead to wait for Vita in Amiens. Denys confronted Vita while she was still hanging about waiting for a boat, and she confessed what was going on. He decided to travel across with her and perform the heavy husband act in Amiens. By this time, George Keppel, Violet's father had also turned up. He insisted on joining them, and, on reaching Amiens, created a scene and refused to go back without his daughter.

The whole thing was too much, even for the ardent lovers. Violet felt they had been defeated by the forces of convention and finally agreed they had better go home. She continued to bombard Vita with letters and for a long time she and Denys hardly spoke to each other, but the great scandal was nearly over.

At the end of 1920 Violet was still passionately in love, but Vita was cooling off. By the end of 1922 Vita was looking back on the whole affair as a madness of which she would never again be capable, though she was on the brink of meeting Virginia Woolf . . .

The patience of Denys Trefusis was finally rewarded. Once the affair with Vita had died down they discovered they liked being married. They never had children but they had lots of things in common, loved literature and travel and had the same sense of humour. They lived in Paris together until his tragically early death from tuberculosis in 1929.

Violet still had another lifetime to live. She became a novelist, a great hostess and a focus of Paris intellectual society. Colette re-named her 'Geranium'. She did become a very close friend of the Princess de Polignac, who, as all the world knew, had tastes in a certain direction, but who preferred to keep her private life very private indeed. Violet, having had a taste of social ruin, decided in future to do the same. She died, considered by everybody a grand old lady, on 1 March 1972. She was 79.

Messalina

The Roman Empire, in its heyday, produced a bevy of women whose exploits chilled the blood. Livia, Agrippina and Poppaea were bad enough, But the monster of them all was Messalina, wife of the gentle Emperor, Claudius.

Her power over him was such that for years he went in ignorance of her cruelty, debauchery and avarice. When he began to suspect the truth, he was too timid to act. Beautiful to look at, she always knew how to soothe and flatter him, how to twist the truth and lull his fears.

Her education in the darker side of life began very early for her mother, Lepida, was a vicious woman who dabbled in magic as well as prostitution and carried on an incestuous relationship with her own brother.

Messalina married Claudius before he became Emperor. She was his fifth wife. They had a daughter, Octavia, later to marry the Emperor Nero and a son, Britannicus, born within the first few weeks of his reign. But she was a woman of such passionate desires that she could never remain faithful.

Claudius became Emperor in a coup that surprised him as much as the rest of Rome. He was bookish, some thought simple, with an easy, indolent nature, much addicted to the pleasures of eating and gaming. Every day he gave sumptuous feasts to which as many as 600 people were invited. He never troubled his head about what was going on in his household.

His wife, with her silky brown limbs and provocative eyes, had no difficulty attracting lovers. Only later, when her true nature was known, did those who were fascinated by her, think twice. When she first became Empress she carried on her love affairs secretly and with discretion but as she began to realize that no one dared oppose her, she flaunted her passions as she chose.

Ironically, her cruelty was first brought to light by a fit of jealousy. Her victim was Princess Julia, daughter of Germanicus and sister of the terrifying Caligula. This Princess and her sister had been banished by Caligula to the island of Pontia after he had abused and raped them both. Claudius, touched by their plight, recalled them from exile and restored them to their estates and former splendour.

Julia was a fascinating woman but unfortunately, as it turned out, being descended from the Caesars, had inherited a haughtiness and noble bearing which Messalina detested. It was also obvious that the Emperor seemed to have a great regard for her and they spent a lot of time together.

Mistaking her husband's regard for love, Messalina began to look upon the handsome Julia as a rival to be got rid of. She brought about her downfall by accusing her of crimes she could not possibly have committed. Claudius believed what he was told and Julia was banished. Soon after, through Messalina's agency, she was killed.

From now on anyone who stood in her way became the victim of her cruelty. She had only to accuse them of treason or an equal crime, and they were put to death without mercy. Her word became law. Appius Silanus was one of the first to die in this way. He had married her mother, Lepida, and become a close friend to Claudius. He was universally well thought of and expected to achieve high office. But he had the misfortune to be found attractive by Messalina. She made advances to him which he repelled, reminding her of their family relationship. Humiliated, she swore to destroy him.

Claudius had a superstitious belief in dreams so when Messalina's servant, Narcissus, told him, on her instructions, of a dream in which he saw Silanus plunge a dagger into the Emperor's heart, he was disturbed. It only needed Messalina to add that she too had had the same dream several nights in succession, and Claudius fell into the trap set for him. Believing he was about to be assassinated, he gave orders for Silanus to be killed.

This served as a strong warning to the senate as to what they could expect from their Emperor under the spell of his evil wife. Several leading senators determined to get rid of Claudius and had plans for the Emperor of Dalmatia, with his vast army, to take over in Rome.

The plans came to nothing, but gave Messalina the opportunity for the violence she had been waiting for. Claiming to be acting for the good of the state she hunted down the guilty senators, in Claudius' name. Estates were confiscated, men tortured, anyone remotely connected with the plot put to death. Things came to such a pitch that many preferred to commit suicide rather than risk capture. She was intoxicated by her power and had reached a point at which she believed the least resistance to her should be punished.

She had a ravenous physical appetite, and heaped rewards on those who joined her in debauchery. Not being content with her own degredation, she forced women of rank to prostitute themselves. If they refused, she had them raped in front of their husbands. She ordered a room in the palace to be fitted up like a brothel, had the name of the most notorious whore in Rome inscribed over the top and amused herself by impersonating her, giving herself to every man that came.

Her infamy was common knowledge yet, incredibly, kept from Claudius. Messalina could make him believe what she wanted to and sometimes made a fool of him. This was so in the affair of Mnester, the most famous dancer in Rome. She was so madly in love with him that she had statues of him erected all over the city, but he did not give in to her being afraid of what would happen to him if the Emperor found out. She pursued him until at last he said he would do whatever she pleased as long as the Emperor consented. Messalina went to Claudius and 'after a thousand deceitful caresses' complained that Mnester had refused to obey her over some petty business. She asked Claudius to give directions that her orders were to be treated with more respect. Claudius sent for the dancer and told him, in future, to obey Messalina implicitly. He obeyed and became her lover.

Greed was another of her vices. For years she had coveted the beautiful Gardens of Lucullus owned by Asiaticus, a senator of great distinction. As she

Messalina

could get them no other way she accused him of being responsible for Caligula's murder, saying he had boasted of the asassination. To everyone, it was obvious he was innocent, but by trickery she had him condemned and he was forced to choose his own death.

There was still one more outrage for her to commit – but it was the one which brought about her end. Passionately in love, yet again, she saw no reason why she should not have two husbands. Her lover was Gaius Silius, a strikingly handsome man who had already been appointed Consul for the following year. By now, drunk with power, she decided to marry him in public and forced him to send away his own wife.

She heaped honours and favours upon this 'husband to be' and stripped the palace of costly hangings, furniture, silver and statues to enrich his house. Silius himself, now trapped, was far from easy in his mind. Although bewitched by the Emperor's wife, he was increasingly aware of the danger to which he was exposing himself.

Messalina chose a weekend when Claudius was away in the country for the celebration of their wedding. It was an affair of great magnificence for which she was dressed as a bride and the feast which followed it went on for days. Claudius knew nothing of it. The truth was broken to him through Narcissus, Messalina's former servant, who hated her and vowed to ruin her. Silius, he was warned, was practically Emperor and Rome in chaos. His initial astonishment and fear gave way to rage. His friends warned him to deal with the couple at once and ensure his safety.

Word soon got back to Rome that Claudius was coming to punish his wife. Hoping to move him to compassion, Messalina sent their children, Octavia and Britannicus, to meet him. She was still sure she could save herself if only she could be alone with him. Narcissus made sure they did not meet. He took the Emperor to see the love nest, sumptuously furnished with his own fine things. Silius was put to death immediately.

But Claudius did not act instantly with regard to his wife. He ordered her to present herself next morning to justify her behaviour. Those around him decided they must act. Centurions were ordered, in the name of the Emperor to find her and put her to death.

Messalina had fled to the Gardens of Lucullus. Her mother, Lepida, was with her. The centurions broke open the gates of the garden and the captain presented himself to her, without a word. He handed her a dagger, giving her the chance to kill herself but she couldn't do it. To make an end of it quickly, he ran her through with his sword.

Claudius was given news of her death but did not seem to take it in. For some time after he would plaintively ask why the Empress Messalina did not come.

Jane Digby

English aristocrat, Jane Digby, shocked her upper class world to the core by collecting and discarding husbands at an alarming rate before finally disappearing into the desert to marry a Bedouin sheik.

An exquisite woman with a streak of high spirited wildness, she didn't give a fig for convention and as a result lived one of the most scandalous lives of the 19th century.

The Digbys knew when their daughter blossomed from a tomboy into a raving beauty with pale gold hair, deep violet eyes, creamy complexion and a perfect figure, that she was going to be a handful. Not only was her beauty obvious by the time she was 13, but so was her power to attract men. At a family conference at Holkham Hall in Norfolk, it was decided she should be married off as soon as possible to keep her out of mischief.

Whoever became her husband had a daunting pedigree to live up to. She was a descendant of two extraordinary families; the Digbys, whose line could be traced back to Edward the Confessor, and the Cokes, whose roots went back to King John and the Magna Carta. Her father, Captain Henry Digby was a hero of Trafalgar but it was the enormous wealth of her mother's family, the Cokes, that had built palatial Holkham Hall in north Norfolk where Jane spent her childhood.

When she was 16 she was taken to London for her coming out season. At the great ball given in her honour in the spring of 1824 she met Edward Law, second Lord Ellenborough, who was regarded by everyone as a splendid 'catch'. Certainly he was a handsome man of distinguished bearing, wealthy, ambitious, respected. The fact that he was a widower more than twice her age, vain, lacking in warmth and, for all his brilliance, generally disliked by his peers, did not seem to worry anyone.

Jane was flattered by his proposal and agreed to marry him.

She had obviously imagined that being Lady Ellenborough would mean having a fine London house, taking her place as a leading hostess, constant dinner parties and balls. But once the honeymoon was over Lord Ellenborough went back to his politics and his sophisticated friends, leaving his beautiful child-wife – she was barely 17 – to pine with boredom at his country house in Roehampton.

He was generous enough and humoured her whims but otherwise condemned her to a life of paying calls and choosing dresses. Sometimes she attended grand receptions on his arm when she would bare her bosom as

Jane Digby

much as she dared. He seems to have married her for two reasons – to provide him with a decorative partner when necessary and to give him a son and heir. Once the latter was achieved he left her more or less alone and they moved into separate bedrooms.

But if her distinguished husband was cold, Jane Digby was made of fire and passion and soon turned elsewhere for consolation. Since childhood she had been half in love with her first cousin, George Anson, and it was probably with him she first deceived Ellenborough. Then, before she had been married three years, she went to stay at Holkham Hall where she found a handsome young scholar an official of the British Museum, in residence engaged in the tedious job of cataloguing the famous Long Library. She wooed him with her violet eyes, then seduced him and it was only when his journals were unsealed in 1920 that the story of their affair was told and the young librarian revealed as the future Sir Frederick Madden.

Back in London, with her husband's approval, she began to attend the fashionable Wednesday Night Balls, held under the patronage of great hostesses such as Lady Jersey and Princess Esterhazy. He would escort Jane to the door of the ballroom then leave to spend his evening elsewhere discussing politics. One night she was introduced to Prince Felix Schwarzenberg the newly arrived Austrian attaché. She took one look at him and was hypnotised. He was her idea of a perfect Byronic hero, strikingly good looking with a thick black moustache, dark eyes, magnificent shoulders and an air of mystery that was magnetic. Schwarzenberg had arrived in London with a reputation as a heart breaker of international repute, but she ignored all warnings. Her intense passion for him was evident from the moment they danced together and he was captivated by her. Almost daily during the summer of 1828 they were seen together. Her elegant green phaeton, drawn by sleek, black ponies, would take her from Roehampton to the Prince's rooms in Harley Street and sometimes they even dared to slip away to Brighton for a weekend rendezvous.

Whether Lord Ellenborough had decided not to notice or whether he was too busy with his political ambitions to care, no one was quite sure, but soon gossip about the two lovers was so flagrant that the Austrian Ambassador, Prince Esterhazy, began to concern himself. What if Ellenborough suddenly woke up to what was going on. The public scandal would do irreparable harm. Schwarzenberg, being warned, decided to safeguard himself by starting another flirtation. His reputation being what it was, nobody was in the least bit surprised, but as it turned out, it was the worst thing he could have done. Jane complained loudly and tearfully to half London that she had been abandoned by her lover until Prince Esterhazy, in desperation, had the amorous attaché recalled to Vienna.

Pandemonium followed. Jane, finding she was three months pregnant with his child planned to leave Lord Ellenborough and accompany her lover to Vienna. This was not quite as he saw it. Begging her to make things up with her husband, he headed for the nearest Channel port. Ellenborough, having been told everything, and with one eye on the premiership, decided he would have to divorce Jane to save his honour.

The Digbys and Cokes, nearly prostrate with shock over the disgrace, descended on Roehampton *en masse* and tried to persuade their erring beauty to beg her husband's forgiveness. She would not, of course, do anything of the sort. Her parents were appalled.

Now in Vienna, a thoroughly embarrassed Prince Schwarzenberg was trying to persuade his ardent mistress to stay where she was. He could never marry her, he pointed out, because of the scandal! However he could not ignore her passionate entreaties for ever and eventually promised that if she left England and took up residence in Basle, he would look after her and the child. So, on the last day of August 1829 Jane Digby sailed from England. Ellenborough was unusually generous in the allowance he gave her saying that he did not want her to be without those comforts and conveniences to which her rank in life entitled her. The Ellenborough's divorce caused a sensation and because of the distaste for such procedures in 19th century England, it needed a private act of parliament before it was declared fully legal.

Jane gave birth to a daughter, Mathilde, in November that year. When the Prince was sent to serve with the Austrian Embassy in Paris he weakened and decided to take his beautiful mistress with him. She lived stylishly enough, first in the Faubourg St Germain, later in the Place du Palais, but because of her situation could not be received in the best circles. Jane became pregnant again and gave birth to a son, who died, but if there was ever a faint hope that the Prince might marry her then, it was soon crushed by the Schwarzenberg family which regarded her as a shameless English baggage.

Soon the Prince's name was being linked with other women in Paris and after a violent quarrel at the Place du Palais one night he left without a word of farewell, and arranged to be sent home to Bavaria. It was obviously the excuse he had been waiting for to extricate himself from the affair.

Desperate about what to do next, Jane arranged to meet her mother, Lady Andover, to discuss possibilities. The distraught parent suggested Munich where the family had connections. But on no account was she to return to England and embarrass everyone.

Jane made a splendid start in Germany by catching the eye of King Ludwig I of Bavaria who had made a life long habit of collecting beautiful women and now fell madly in love with her. At the same time she accepted the passionate courtship of a great landowner, Baron Karl Venningen who escorted her to the opera, the balls, the outdoor cafés, all the public places where the King could not be seen with her. Between swooning over the memory of Schwarzenberg and dallying with the King, she drove poor Venningen half crazy. But when she became pregnant again – the third time without a husband – and he proposed marriage, she agreed.

For a time she enjoyed the security and acceptance that came with being known as 'the beautiful Baroness von Venningen' but after only a year there were signs of friction. Jane continued to be on intimate terms with the King, and, though never quite sure whether she was his mistress or not, the Baron writhed with jealousy. He took her to live at Weinheim, a secluded, medieval watering spot 11 miles north of Heidelberg, but their relationship was not the sort that thrived on solitude. She became so bored and restless that he gave in to her pleas and took her back to Munich for the season.

Soon, however, both the middle aged king and the gallant baron were to be obscured by the appearance of a dazzling figure rejoicing in the name of Count Spiridion Theotoky. He was only 24, fiery, magnificent to look at and a member of one of the most aristocratic families on the Greek island of Corfu. From the moment Jane saw him at a carnival ball she knew she was on the threshold of another grand passion. As for the Greek, he was enchanted by the wild little Baroness with pale gold hair.

Not daring to breathe her love in daylight she would wait until the household was asleep then saddle her throughbred mare and ride out in the moonlight to meet her 'Spiro'. They made one attempt to elope but the Baron gave chase, hauled Theotoky out of his carriage and challenged him to a duel in which the latter was slightly wounded.

After her dash for freedom, the marriage held together until the spring of 1839 when she fled to Paris with Spiro, leaving behind a heartbroken husband and two children. 'The misfortune of my nature is to consider love is all in all' she wrote to King Ludwig trying to explain her behaviour. As for the Baron, she had to admit he behaved nobly, even offering her his house as a haven should she ever need it. Jane Digby had that effect on people.

To her family this latest affair was the last straw. Her grandfather would not allow her name to be mentioned and though she was reconciled with her mother who could never be cross with her for long, her father, now Admiral Digby, never forgave her and never saw her again.

In Paris she posed first of all as Spiro's niece and later as his wife. In March 1840 she gave birth to his son, Leonidas. Though her other children were scattered around Europe in the care of various relatives, she seemed to cherish this child especially, little knowing how soon she would lose him.

The couple stayed in Paris until the spring of 1841 when with great excitement on Jane's part, they set out for the Greek islands, staying first at Tinos where Spiro's father was governor then carrying on to Corfu to live on the family estates.

Before setting out for the Aegean they wanted to become man and wife. As von Venningen had not even started divorce proceedings they decided to have that marriage dissolved through the Greek Orthodox Church. It is believed they were then married by a Greek Orthodox priest in Marseilles.

They arrived in Corfu as Count and Countess Theotoky. For three years they were blissfully happy there, living in an Italian style villa some twenty miles from the capital where they entertained lavishly and attended all the grand balls and receptions in town.

Their idyll was not to last long. King Otto called Spiro to Athens to become his *aide-de-camp* and the call was mandatory and included Jane. Once again her beauty proved her undoing for the King could not keep his eyes off her. Queen Amalia was furious and took an instant dislike to the Countess Theotoky while Spiro played the offended husband and in retaliation began a series of affairs. For a time it seemed as though their marriage was kept together by only one thing – their mutual love of their son.

Tragedy struck in the summer of 1846. The Theotokys went to their summer house, a tall Florentine villa in the Italian spa town of Bagni di Lucca. It was an imposing house with a reception hall three stories high and inside balconies at all levels. One day, hearing his parents voices in the hall the boy leaned over the balcony railing on the top floor, lost his balance and fell to the black and white marble floor below. He was killed outright at his mother's feet.

Jane never fully recovered. Shattered with grief she believed that his death was a punishment for the way she had neglected her other children. She and Spiro went their separate ways. She disappeared for a time and the rumour was that she took six husbands to console herself, a slander she fervently denied.

By 1849 she was back in Athens and her house became a meeting place for the liveliest and most interesting people of the day. Though she did not know it, the most colourful part of her life was about to begin.

King Otto, who frequently changed his *aides-de-camp*, had given Spiro's post to the most fantastic figure in Greece, the brigand chief, General Cristodoulos Hadji-Petros. This extraordinary man, leader of the fierce band of mountain freedom fighters who initiated the Greek War of Independence and called themselves 'Pallikari' (the brave ones) was nearly 70 but with his sinewy body, shock of white hair and fine moustaches, he carried his age lightly. Jane fell passionately in love with him.

When Cristos was made governor of the mountain province of Lamia, she did not hesitate to sell her house and follow her new lover to his rugged outpost. The life suited her as never before and she revelled in it, wearing coarse cotton smocks like the mountain women and sleeping between rough goats hair blankets as though she had never known the feel of silk. She galloped over the mountains, slept in the open, ate and drank the roughest food. Nothing deterred her as long as she could be with Cristos. Her lover's small government salary was augmented by highway robbery but he was careful to shield her from its more bloody aspects and she accepted it as part of mountain life. She was so happy she could think of nothing better than to be his wife.

Alas, her mountain venture was to last no more than a few months. Word got back to Athens that Countess Theotoky was living openly in the mountains with Hadji-Petros. Squeals of outrage went up from all sides and Queen Amalia, her old enemy, saw a way to avenge herself. She insisted that Cristos be dismissed from government for openly keeping a mistress. The old brigand wrote to the Queen explaining that he had only lived with the Countess for profit, not love – 'She is rich, I am poor. I have a rank to live up to, children to educate. I trust therefore .....' The queen had the note displayed publicly. Jane understood him enough to forgive this piece of ungallantry, but when he started to seduce young women, she felt she had taken enough.

Without notice to anyone, she vanished from Athens, leaving Hadji-Petros and her dream of a mountain marriage behind.

She had been planning a trip to Syria to buy horses and decided to go through with the journey in order to distance herself from the persuasive Cristos. He usually had an explanation for everything and she might be tempted to listen. She sailed for Beirut on 6 April, 1853, three days after her 46th birthday.

During the voyage she decided to give herself up to travel, to see as much as she could of the Middle East and perhaps even join a desert caravan. But before she could set out for Palmyra or Petra, a young Bedouin sheik came into her life.

She was still as vulnerable to passion as she had been as a girl of 17. When she first saw Saleh against the background of low, black Bedouin tents she knew she would fall in love with him. She had been taken out to the encampment in the desert to buy a horse but dealing was soon forgotten. Saleh saw before him a beautiful, mature woman, and was fascinated.

Before the dealing was through he had invited her to his tent.

Jane became totally infatuated with Saleh, though he was twenty years younger than she was. She recognized something in the Arab of her own nature. She made up her mind she was going to marry him and embrace the Bedouin culture.

She had to return to Athens to settle her affairs and her friends threw up their hands in horror when they learned she was considering marriage to a Bedouin Arab. She could hardly wait to get back to him. She raced across the desert only to find, to her horror, that her place in his tent had been taken by a beautiful dark eyed girl called Sabla, a brown nymph scarcely more than a child.

Jane realized that her passionately romantic nature had led her into one affair too many. As she turned back towards Damascus she determined to eliminate men from her life altogether. But there was still one more to come, and that worth all the rest.

Shortly after she had met and fallen in love with Saleh, she made plans to visit the ancient ruins of Palmyra. For this an escort was essential and the British Consul in Damascus told her to contact the Mesrab Arabs who for centuries had controlled the stretch of desert on the way to Palmyra. A younger son of their great sheik was sent to negotiate with her. His name was Medjuel el Mesrab. He was slight, graceful with a handsome olive face and dark beard; he could not only read and write but spoke several languages and was an authority on desert history.

In short he was a true aristocrat. By the end of their journey, which took them through dangerous territory and demanded cool nerves, Medjuel was full of admiration for the beautiful English woman. He admired her so much in fact that he asked her to marry him but at the time she had thoughts for no one but Saleh.

Now on her way back to Damascus she thought about Medjuel again. He had never forgotten her, never taken another woman and never given up hope of marrying her. Hearing that Madame Digby, as he called her, was in the caravan approaching Damascus he set out to meet her with a valuable Arab mare as a gift of welcome.

A few months later they were married.

Jane made one more journey home in the autumn of 1856 mostly for the purpose of being reconciled with her mother but English society found her marriage to an Arab when she still had three husbands living, too much to accept. She met members of her family but felt at a distance from them. Victorian England was no place for her and after six months she kissed her mother goodbye for the last time and set off back to her spiritual home with a flock of Norfolk turkeys for her beloved Medjuel and ammunition for her Bedouin tribe.

She spent the rest of her life with him, sometimes in the desert as a Bedouin wife but mostly in a charming house he bought for her in Damascus and where she received many English visitors. Most of all she loved riding by his side out into the desert and for her 73rd birthday in 1880 he brought her the most beautiful horse she had ever seen.

Only twelve months later, in August 1881 she fell ill with a virulent dysentry. Medjuel sat by her bed as she grew weaker day by day. When she died he obeyed her last wishes and she was buried in the Protestant cemetery in Damascus. Then, the grief stricken Bedouin rode out to the desert and sacrificed one of his finest camels to her memory.

Caroline of Brunswick

On the morning of George IV's coronation his wife, Caroline of Brunswick, rose from her bed at dawn, put on robes of white satin, pinned white ostrich plumes in her hair then drove to Westminster Abbey, where the door was shut in her face.

'I am your Queen,' cried Caroline, 'Will you not admit me?' and Lord Hood, who was among those who had accompanied her, on being asked for a pass replied huffily: 'I present you your Queen – surely there is no need for her to have a ticket.'

But in spite of this farcical exchange, the party got no further. Orders had been given that on no account was Caroline to be allowed over the threshold. Inside, the Coronation went on without her. Prinny had won his battle against the wife he detested. Now she would never be crowned.

The most extraordinary marriage in the history of British royalty started to go wrong the moment the couple met. The Prince of Wales took one look at the short, bosomy German girl who had been chosen for him, walked sharply to the other end of the room and whispered to his friend the Earl of Malmesbury 'Harris, I am not well, pray get me a glass of brandy.'

Caroline was astonished, but did not collapse in tears as many would have done. 'Mon Dieu!' she exclaimed in a loud voice. 'Is the Prince always like that. I find him very fat and nothing like as handsome as his portraits.'

That was the trouble with Caroline. She never knew when to keep her mouth shut. The Prince was fastidious, vain, sensitive. She was totally opposite. Her behaviour was like that of a hoydenish schoolgirl, lacking in feminine grace, with a freakish sense of humour and brashness which sealed her fate as far as the Prince was concerned. Little did he know the chaos she was to bring into his life, though most people felt they deserved each other.

Her parents, the Duke and Duchess of Brunswick, found her an odd, precocious child from the very beginning. There was a wildness about her which defied discipline and she told terrible lies.

When she was 16 she was quite a pretty girl with powdered curls, soft skin and bright eyes. But her behaviour was awful. Having been forbidden to attend a court ball by her mother, she retired to bed screaming that she was pregnant and about to give birth. All havoc was let loose and the midwife fetched. 'Now Madam,' said the Princess to her swooning mother 'Will you forbid me to go to a ball again?'

At 26 she was still unmarried. Eligible princes who had been considered for her were amused by her company but fled at the hint of a wedding. When, therefore, in 1794, the Duke was asked for Caroline's hand on behalf of the Prince of Wales, he was overjoyed. The Prince had never set eyes on her and had already contracted an unlawful marriage with a Catholic widow, Maria Fitzherbert, with whom he was very much in love. But his debts, due to over rich living and gambling were phenomenal and the King, anxious for his son to produce an heir, promised to wipe them out provided he would take a lawful wife. Caroline seemed eminently suitable as a Princess from a staunch Protestant family.

Lord Malmesbury was sent to fetch her. He tried hard to see her better points. She could be very kind and was good natured on the whole. But, he had to admit, she was also far too easy in her manners, familiar and coarse. He tried to give her lessons in court dignity and to make her aware of the importance of being Princess of Wales. But the fact that worried him most was that Caroline was not very clean, for the dandified Prince was always immaculate. Caroline didn't wash very often and wore coarse underclothes and thick stockings which were seldom laundered. What's more it seemed to be a subject on which she was singularly obtuse.

On arrival in England she was taken over by the bossy Lady Jersey, the Prince's favourite, who supervised her toilette and dressed her up like a Christmas chicken for that disastrous first meeting with the Prince. Caroline hated her and soon reverted to her old style.

The wedding took place in the Chapel Royal at St James's Palace on 8 April 1795. The Prince was deathly pale and only got through the ceremony with regular prompting from the King. He apparently spent the greater part of his wedding night snoring in the fireplace 'Where he fell, and I left him' as Caroline told everybody afterwards. There was no doubt he found her physically repellant and stayed in bed only long enough to consummate the marriage.

When it became obvious that Caroline was 'wid child' as she put it, she roared 'I don't believe it' and suggested slyly that the Prince was not capable of fatherhood, a slur he never forgave her.

She gave birth to a daughter, Princess Charlotte, on 7 January 1796 and her husband wrote in his diary 'The Princess was brought to bed of an *immense* girl.' Of course he wanted a boy so that the whole thing was over and done with. The disappointment brought on one of his fits of hypochondria and he felt so miserable that he thought he must be dying. He made his will, leaving everything to Mrs Fitzherbert and stating that the care of his daughter should be in the hands of the King. 'The mother of this child', he wrote, 'is to have no hand in her upbringing.' He went on: 'The convincing and repeated proofs I have received of her entire lack of judgement and of feeling, make me

Princess Caroline

deem it incumbent upon me to prevent by all possible means, the child falling into such improper and bad hands as hers. . . .'

After the birth of Charlotte they drew further and further apart. The Prince, who complained to his mother of her 'personal nastiness' – in other words she stank – would not even eat with her. He occupied one wing of Carlton House, his vast London home, the Princess another and the royal baby with its army of nannies, a third.

The Prince was beginning to say openly that he despaired of the relationship ever settling down and in the end wrote to Caroline 'Nature has not made us suitable to each other, but to be tranquil and comfortable is, however, within our power; let our intercourse therefore be restricted. . . .' And they agreed to separate.

Princess Caroline set up her own household at Montague House, Blackheath and rumours soon began to spread about the wild parties she held there. She invited naval officers from nearby Greenwich, including the famous Admiral Sir Sidney Smith and Captain Manby, a frigate commander. One servant claimed she had seen her mistress in such an indecent situation with Sir Sidney that she fainted! Caroline had taken a dislike to English women, so many of her parties were all male. She had a habit of disappearing with her favourite in tow, leaving her guests to fend for themselves. 'I have a bedfellow whenever I like' she told a friend. She also exposed her bosom more than was thought decent and would dance about, exposing her garters when the mood took her.

Soon people began to refuse her invitations. When one of her ladies-in-waiting dared to suggest that she was going too far, Caroline turned on her in a fury and dismissed her for impudence.

At Blackheath Caroline struck up a friendship with her neighbour, Lady Charlotte Douglas, a fine looking woman with a taste for scandal and indecency that equalled her own. The friendship was to cost Caroline dear and to lead to an humiliating investigation into her love life.

The trouble started when Lady Charlotte announced that she was expecting a child. Caroline, who was beginning to weary of her friend decided to play a prank on her. She too would be pregnant. She stuffed her dresses with cushions and began to crave fried onion rings at breakfast. After a suitable time, when her Ladyship called one day, Caroline showed her a sleeping baby boy. Only when she had had her full quota of fun from Lady Charlotte's discomfort did she tell her the full story. Her Ladyship was not amused.

The boy's name, apparently, was William Austin, and he was the son of a Deptford dock labourer. One of Caroline's better habits had been to help poor and orphaned children and Mrs Austin, hearing of her good works in this direction and her husband having lost his job, pleaded for her help. Caroline offered to take her baby boy. He arrived just in time for her prank, but was to stay close to her for the rest of her life.

She called him 'Little Willum' and when someone referred to him as 'Your son' she cried 'Prove it and he shall be your King.' This, of course, was dangerous talk and got back to the Prince of Wales, who wanted to know what on earth was going on.

Lady Charlotte saw how to have her revenge. She was furious with Caroline for dropping her and also for her affair with Sir Sidney Smith. She had once been his mistress. She declared that Caroline had secretly given birth to 'Little Willum' in 1802. She also gave a list of her lovers.

It was obvious something had to be done. 'So much levity and profligacy....' moaned the old King George III, who was thought to be tottering on the brink of his sanity. In 1806 a commission of inquiry was appointed to discuss Caroline's behaviour – it was called the Delicate Investigation. Only when Sophia Austin, the baby's real mother, was interviewed, was the Princess cleared of adultery. The royal commissioners censured her over 'other particulars of her conduct' and she was rebuked by the King (but he had a soft spot for her and quite enjoyed a boisterous day at her house in Blackheath.)

After the investigation, Caroline was determined to be reinstated at Court and declared she would fight the whole royal family if need be. Her appearance at the King's birthday celebrations was not a success. She had grown fat, went without corsets, and dressed gaudily, showing too much bosom. The temperature was distinctly chilly and the Prince kept away from her.

But whatever Caroline's faults, people throughout the country had sympathy for her over one thing: the enforced separation from her daughter, Charlotte. Ever since she moved to Blackheath they had only been allowed fortnightly meetings. But an incident occurred when Princess Charlotte was 16 that convinced many people that the Prince of Wales had acted wisely. The young girl fell in love with a Lieutenant Hesse of the 18th Light Dragoons. He was rumoured to be the Duke of York's illegitimate son. Although her lady-in-waiting, Lady de Clifford, knew the affair should be stopped, Caroline thoroughly approved. She considered that at 16 a girl should take her first lessons in love and acted as their go-between. She arranged meetings for them and, when they paid her secret visits at her apartments in Kensington Palace she would lead them to her bedroom, turn back the bedcovers and lock the door. What really pleased her was the thought of hoodwinking the Prince of Wales. Fortunately for her, Hesse turned out to be a gentleman and did not take advantage of the situation, and the Prince did not find out.

With the turn of history, things were to become much more difficult for her. On 6 February 1811, the King being desperately ill, the Prince of Wales was sworn in as Regent and in effect began his reign. A year later the King was pronounced incurable and he took over full powers. Almost the first thing he did was to further restrict meetings between his wife and daughter.

Caroline, furious, published a highly indiscreet letter stating all her grievances in high flown language. She gained unexpected support. The Whigs, who had been led to believe they would take office when the Prince succeeded, had been badly let down. He kept the Tories in power to please his new mistress, Lady Hertford. To show their disgust, the Whigs decided to champion Caroline. Suddenly she had a following. Loyal addresses began to arrive from all over the country and the Lord Mayor of London paid her a call.

The Regent, with new evidence up his sleeve, petulantly ordered another investigation into her morals. Twenty-three privy councillors were appointed to go through all the sordid details but the outcome was much as before. Caroline treated it as a triumph and was cheered in the streets.

But while the investigation was going on she was not allowed to see Charlotte at all. From then on, mother and daughter were to meet only by accident. There was just one final scene between them in July 1813. Charlotte had broken off her engagement to the Prince of Orange, her excuse being that she must stay in England to be near her mother. The Prince suspected her of being in love with someone else and, in a temper, planned to close down her London household and send her to a lodge in the middle of Windsor Forest. Charlotte took refuge with the only person she knew who would defy her father – Caroline. But she had chosen a bad time. Her mother had plans of her own. Charlotte was persuaded to return to her father and obey his wishes. Mother and daughter never met again.

Caroline had decided to travel. She was now 46, had endured England for 19 years and decided she had suffered enough humiliation. She wanted to enjoy herself. The Prince, only too glad to see her go, arranged for a frigate to take her across the Channel with her entourage, which included a pale youth of 13 – William Austin. She left with untypical dignity wearing a sombre, military style overcoat. As she watched the coast off England recede, she fainted with emotion.

Waiting on the other side was a bizarre collection of horse drawn vehicles followed by an old London to Dover mail coach intended to carry servants and baggage. The party called first at Brunswick, where Caroline was well received by her elder brother, the Duke, then went on to Switzerland and Italy.

The behaviour of the Princess grew wilder and wilder. When she was warned that her indiscretions were being reported back in England she laughed. 'The Regent will hear it, as you say: I hope he will. I love to mortify him.' Most of the English aristocrats in her entourage went home. They couldn't stand the pace.

Caroline had taken to wearing a black wig which did not suit her. Lady Bessborough, who caught sight of her at a ball in Genoa wrote: 'I cannot tell you how sorry and asham'd I felt as an Englishwoman. The first thing I saw in the room was a short, very fat, elderly woman, with an extremely red face (owing I suppose to the heat) in a girl's white dress, but with shoulder, back and neck quite low (disgustingly so) down to the middle of her stomach; very black hair and eyebrows, which gave her a fierce look, and a wreath of light pink roses on her head...'

While she was in Milan Caroline engaged an Italian called Bartolomeo Pergami to be her courier. He was a splendid looking man, who had fought for Napoleon, and he was rapidly promoted from being a servant to something far more intimate. Her long suffering lady-in-waiting, Lady Charlotte Campbell, considered this the last straw and was regretfully 'obliged to resign.' Before long most of Pergami's relatives had joined the household, which was now almost entirely Italian. What Caroline did not realize was that her husband had spies everywhere, trying to catch her in the act which would give him his divorce.

She was having a marvellous time in Italy and was completely infatuated by Pergami. She bought the Villa d'Este on the shore of Lake Como for herself, and for him she purchased a small estate, south of Catania, carrying with it the title of Baron de la Francine. Full of high spirits, Caroline took her motley courtiers on to Sicily, where she had to be dissuaded from climbing a rumbling Mount Etna, then to Tunis, where she was received by the Bey and then on to the Holy Land, where she created the Order of St Caroline and made Pergami the Grand Master.

Caroline and Pergami were obviously living as man and wife. At the Villa d'Este his sitting room was next to hers, his bedroom the only one near hers. His picture was in every room. There were rumours that the Pergami family were swindling her with impunity.

Caroline was on her way to Rome when the news came through that George III was dead. With emotion she realized that she was now Queen of England. The Prince Regent, at the age of 47, was at last to ascend the throne.

She demanded a meeting with Lord Henry Brougham, who had always been sympathetic to her and they met on neutral ground in France, at St Omer on the way to Calais. He had been told to offer Caroline an annual allowance of £50,000 to give up her crown. She refused it, with disdain. Brougham pleaded with her to return quietly and secretly, if she must. But Caroline had been waiting for this moment for years and was not going to be done out of it.

The Prince Regent was far from popular. His insane spending at a time when the poorer classes were at starvation level made many people despise him. But when Caroline arrived at Dover she was met by cheering crowds and accorded a 21 gun salute. She was treated as a heroine as she rode into London with William Austin by her side. 'Long live the Queen,' yelled the mob 'and long live King Austin!' The King, appalled at this treachery retired to Windsor with the rest of the royal family.

But before his departure he set in motion yet another investigation into his wife's morals – this time with the hope of gaining a divorce. He had been collecting scandalous information about her goings on in Italy for about five years. Combined with what was known of her intimacy with Pergami he felt sure he could prevent her from becoming Queen.

This time the hearing took place in the House of Lords.

On the day of the hearing, the Court was in mourning for the Duchess of York so Caroline could not put on a show, as she would have liked. She appeared sombrely dressed in a large black bonnet with ostrich plumes and a dress of black figured gauze with white bishop's sleeves and a frilled ruff at the neck. She was given a comfortable chair and a footstool, but could take no part in what was going on.

As it had been agreed that the King could not take direct divorce action against the Queen, the Prime Minister, digging in the archives, had produced an alternative – a Bill of Pains and Penalties. This was an obscure process which could, if the allegations against her were proved to be true, bring about an act of Parliament with the forfeiture of her rights and the end of the royal marriage.

When the proceedings opened with a reading of this Bill, the grounds for the dissolution of the royal marriage were given as a most unbecoming and degrading intimacy between the Queen and one Bartolomeo Pergami, a foreigner of low station.'

The hearing went on for forty days and wore everbody out but the public lapped up every scandalous detail and rolled in the aisles at the spectacle of the monarchy laundering its dirty linen.

One by one, Italian witnesses who had been paid good money to 'tell all' gave graphic accounts of Caroline receiving Pergami at her toilette in only her pantaloons, of Pergami visiting her in nothing more than a silk dressing gown; of Caroline being found asleep with her hand on his private parts and of the pair of them playing silly games wearing nothing but fig leaves.

The intimacy was undeniable. The prosecution did a devastating job but then Lord Brougham took the stand in her defence and spoke for eight hours, by which time people were ready to agree to anything. His final point was astounding in the circumstances. The Queen, he thundered, could not have committed adultery with Pergami. The poor man was impotent. Smitten in his private parts while fighting for Napoleon!

On Friday, 10 November, after a third reading, the vote was taken. Caroline had won – 108 in her favour, 99 against. Scenes of wild excitement broke out and congratulations poured in from all over the country. The King continued to sulk at Windsor but his supporters soon had all London singing this ditty:

> 'Most gracious Queen, we thee implore
> To go away and sin no more
> Or if that effort be too great
> To go away at any rate.'

Flushed with Victory, Caroline informed the Dean of St Paul's that she intended to give thanks in his church for what had taken place. She arrived in procession, watched by a vast crowd, while the King hid himself and tried to puzzle out how he could get rid of her before the Coronation. To his immense relief, the Privy Council met and decided that as Caroline was living apart from His Majesty, she had no right to take part in the ceremony and the King could refuse her the crown.

By the beginning of 1821 the Queen was not as popular with the fickle crowds that had cheered her in the streets. Living at Brandenburg House she lay in bed complaining of the British climate and drinking too much brandy. She had been pestering the King with appeals to let her attend the Coronation, but he refused point blank. He was terrified that she would make a scene.

So, on 19 July 1821, ignoring the pleas of her advisers, she put on her finery and drove to the Abbey....

Not many people noticed her depart. They were too interested in the magnificent show George IV was putting on for their benefit. His robes alone were known to have cost £24,000.

Soon after the Coronation she went to Drury Lane Theatre with a group of friends. During the performance she was taken ill, though she refused to leave until the end. She looked haggard and was obviously in great pain. Her doctor diagnosed obstruction of the bowel and she went into a swift decline. Lord Brougham, who had spoken in her defence, was with her. She told him: 'I am going to die Brougham, but it does not signify.' She had no regrets.

But it was her own daughter, Princess Charlotte, who probably summed up her life best: 'My mother was wicked,' she wrote 'but she would not have turned so wicked had not my father been much more wicked still!'

Chapter Three

Thieves and Outlaws

When women set themselves outside the law they can often prove to be as tough as any man. From the days of the pirate queens to the present era of international terrorism they have played a ruthless part....

Mary Frith

When Mary Frith strode through the streets of 17th century London with her great mastiff 'Wildbrat' panting at her heels, people would step into the gutter to let her pass. A huge woman with a glittering eye and the air of a pirate, dressed like a man and smoking like a chimney she was obviously someone to be reckoned with. The London underworld knew her well enough, but by another name. This was the notorious Moll Cutpurse, queen of the pickpockets, fearless highway robber and receiver of stolen goods.

No one expected Mary to turn out as she did. The only daughter of an honest shoemaker, she was born in 1584, near the Barbican at the upper end of Aldersgate Street. Her parents doted on her and prepared to give her a good education and find her a well-to-do husband. But from the earliest days she proved hard to handle. She hated sewing and stitching, found the company of girls boring and would tear off her white linen cap and apron so that she could fight and sport with boys in the street. Her temper was unruly and she swore like a trooper. Her poor parents must have wondered what they had produced but as someone at the time remarked they were spared the worst as they died in her youth.

Mary grew into a fine, lusty, plain young woman fit to put out to service, everyone hoped, as she had no money to maintain her without working. But as a domestic she was a disaster. She had no time for children, in fact she hated looking after them. She would lose her temper at the slightest thing then go off to the ale house where she would spend every penny she had, then join in the bawdiest and wildest escapades with a laugh that echoed round half London.

At last, her embarrassed relatives seem to have reached the decision that as nothing would change her they had better be rid of her. She was tricked into going aboard a merchant ship lying off Gravesend but discovered in the nick of time that when it sailed for New England she would be one of the passengers. The night before it was due to leave she jumped overboard and swam ashore determined never to go near her treacherous relations again.

The underworld was waiting with open arms. She fell in first with a group of fortune tellers who travelled about the country reading palms and gazing into crystal balls. But her income from this proved totally inadequate for her tastes. She was far more interested in the gangs of pickpockets and thieves who swooped down on the great fairs and markets like vultures and obviously took home rich pickings.

Once admitted to their ranks she threw off her petticoats for good and took to masculine attire. She realized by now that she was not attractive to the opposite sex, that she had no feminine charm and no hope of a husband. Far better, she reasoned, to wear the trousers that suited her and prove herself the equal of any man. Rumours that she was an hermaphrodite were quite untrue.

Mary Frith soon showed herself superior to most of the petty criminals she associated with for she had a brain and a smattering of education as well as the longest, niftiest fingers in the business. It was the fashion during the early days of the 17th century for men and women to wear a pocket or purse attached to a belt round the waist and it was her extraordinary dexterity in separating these purses from their owners by cutting them off that earned her the name 'Moll Cutpurse'.

Fame came to her quickly for in 1610 there was entered in the register of the stationers' company a book called *The madde pranckes of merry Moll....* written by John Day and she was presented on stage as 'a bold virago straight and tall...' in Middleton's *Roaring Girl*. She lapped this up along with the rich pickings but after a few years, having been in prison several times and burned on the hands as punishment, she decided to leave petty crime and take to the highways.

Moll, as she was known from now on, already had a wide circle of friends among the aristocrats of the road including the legendary highwayman, Captain Hind. She was a staunch, declared Royalist and insisted she would only rob Roundheads or any other enemies of the King. Together she and Captain Hind made a daring attack on a wagon containing pay for Commonwealth soldiers in the neighbourhood of Shotover. At other times she went out alone. Her nerve never failed and she became as feared as any man.

Over the years she relieved her victims of thousands of pounds without turning a hair. Though of huge proportions she was a fine horsewoman and nimble on her feet. Escape was never a problem. Then, one day she took part in the famous hold up of General Fairfax on Hounslow Heath. In the fracas he turned on her. She shot him through the arm then, to stop pursuit, fired on and killed two of his horses. After he had been relieved of his money, Fairfax managed to struggle to the town of Hounslow where some of his officers were quartered and he gave orders that she was to be found at all costs. This time she was out of luck. Her own horse had failed her and she was captured at Turnham Green, carried off to Newgate Prison, tried and condemned. But so rampant was the corruption at the time that she was able to buy her freedom from a prison official with a bribe of £2,000!

Moll bought a house in Fleet Street, only two doors away from the Globe

Mary Frith

Tavern. She preferred to live in the hustle and bustle and never shunned the limelight. An official attempt to shame her failed miserably. One day she was summoned to appear before the Court of Arches to answer a charge of wearing 'indecent and manly apparel'. Her defence was considered inadequate and she was ordered to do penance in a white sheet at St Paul's Cross during a Sunday morning sermon. She turned up in her sheet, wept bitterly and seemed truly contrite until someone discovered she was maudlin drunk having consumed three quarts of sack (white wine) before making her appearance. Those who knew her said they might as well have shamed a black dog as Moll for she would have travelled all through the market towns of England in her penitential habit if she had been offered a fair sum.

As though to thumb her nose at the Court of Arches she made a bet of £20 with a vintner in Cheapside that she would ride astride in breeches and doublet from Charing Cross to Shoreditch. She hired two men to walk in front of her, one with a trumpet, the other with a banner. It was too much for the crowds that watched her brazen progress. They called her 'thou shame of women' and threatened to pull her off her horse. But she won her bet.

The Fairfax disaster had actually scared Moll and she decided to try yet another branch of criminal activity. She became a fence, a receiver of stolen property, and her transactions were on a huge scale. By now she was known to all the greatest rogues in the Kingdom and most of them at one time or another called at her house in Fleet Street. Highwaymen like Hind, Hannam and Crowder even left their booty with her while they went off looking for fresh game along the country roads.

She lived comfortably surrounded by dogs, parrots and ornate gilt mirrors and was 'mightily taken with the pastime of smoking'. She was well dressed and her house was said to be pleasantly, if curiously, decorated and furnished. But perhaps she missed the excitement of the road. She took to displaying stolen goods in her front window. One day a gentleman passing by saw his own watch, of which he had recently been relieved, fetched a constable and took Moll and his watch to court. She was duly committed for trial but when the constable entered the witness box he found the watch in question was missing from his pocket. The jury had no alternative but to let her go free. Her friends were waiting for her. They had, of course, accompanied the constable to the court and simply taken it back again!

In her later years she turned her house into a brothel even though she herself had a reputation for chastity. She procured for either sex and became part of a sordid world which included characters like Aniseed-water Robin who wore skirts and petticoats. Her reason was probably lack of money. Though she had stolen a fortune in her time and was known to have put by £5,000 in gold, she had barely £100 left. She willed £30 to three maids and the rest of her estate to a kinsman called Frith, master of a ship at Rotherhithe, whom she advised to stay at home and get drunk rather than go to sea and be drowned in salt water.

Moll Cutpurse died on 26 July 1659 and was buried in St Bride's churchyard with a marble headstone. It disappeared in the Great Fire of London. Near the time of her death she had given instructions that she was to be buried face down so that she might be as preposterous in her death as she had been in her life.

Belle Starr

In legends of the Wild West, Belle Starr is always depicted as a fascinating hussy who combined sex appeal with bravado – a sort of Cleopatra of the range.

Reality was very different. Although she had herself photographed in velvet gown there was usually a six shooter dangling from her hand. Belle was, in fact, an ugly woman, a horse thief with a venomous disposition, and she takes her place in Western history with the worst of the outlaws.

Born Myra Belle Shirley on 5 February 1848 in a log cabin near Carthage Missouri, her background was surprisingly proper. Her father, John Shirley was an ex-judge, a Virginia aristocrat who survived the Civil War and bought an 800 acre homestead to make a new life for himself in Missouri. Nothing is known of her mother, Elizabeth.

When she was eight Belle was sent with lots of other nice little girls in clean white pinafores, to the Carthage Female Academy where she had a chance to learn from a prospectus offering reading, writing, spelling, grammar, deportment, Greek, Latin and Hebrew. But her studies were violently interrupted when war broke out on the Kansas-Missouri border and marauding gangs set fire to John Shirley's cabin. His son, who had joined a Missouri regiment was killed. The ex-judge decided to move the rest of his family, including Belle, out of trouble and into the state of Texas. The move certainly did not keep Belle out of trouble!

Belle grew up in Scyene, ten miles east of Dallas. By the time she was 18 it became obvious that she was no beauty. It also became obvious that she had a taste for rough company and no respect at all for law and order. Her heroes were all thieves and outlaws who didn't give a damn and got away with murder. It was when she was 18 she met Cole Younger, one of the gang of handsome, laughing brothers who rode the outlaw trail with Jesse James. Cole was on the run after robbing a bank with James in Liberty, Missouri and was planning to hide out in Texas. Belle swore to the end of her life that she gave him shelter and he fathered her first child, a daughter she named Pearl. Younger denied this and utterly rejected Pearl, who was born exactly nine months after they met. She was certainly in love with him then and she never forgot him.

Three years later, in 1869, she had a new lover, a prospector called Jim Reed from Vernon County, Missouri, who had taken to bank and train robbery to boost his income. With Reed and two other outlaws she rode to the North Canadian river country in search of gold. They were unsuccessful

Blue Duck and Belle Starr

until one day a fellow prospector, an old Creek Indian, revealed when he was drunk, that he had 30,000 dollars worth hidden away. They tortured him until he revealed where it was.

When the loot was shared out Belle decided to buy herself some finery and return to Texas in style. She paraded around in a flowing velvet gown and wide brimmed, plumed hat with matching six guns and fine leather boots. She also bought a black mare which she called Venus. In their marvellous *Pictorial History of the Wild West* James D. Horan and Paul Sann say that at the turn of the century there were still residents of Scyene who remembered Belle in her velvet gown, shiny boots and six shooters, riding Venus into town with a riding crop dangling from her wrist.

She presented Jim Reed with a baby boy, Edward, in 1871 but he didn't live long to appreciate his son and heir. He was killed by one of his own murderous gang in a gun fight.

Belle rode out of town, leaving her children with her mother, and joined up with a gang of cattle and horse thieves operating in an area known as the Oklahoma Strip. She hated being without a man for long and a flat faced Indian outlaw with the curious name Blue Duck became her next lover. She soon became undisputed leader of the gang and masterminded all their criminal forays for the next five years.

Blue Duck did not last long. His place was taken by another Indian, a tall, slim Cherokee called Sam Starr. Sam was different from the rest and seemed to have some influence over Belle who was now a leather faced woman of 28 and notoriously hard to handle. She married him and when they weren't out on the rampage, rustling and stealing cattle and horses, they lived in a log cabin with a sloping roof near Fort Smith, Arkansas. Belle, in memory of the man she couldn't forget called it Younger's Bend. She acquired some pretty awful relations by her marriage to Sam Starr. One was a terrible old man called Uncle Tom who boasted that he had burned a whole family to death in his heyday.

Younger's Bend became a hideout for some of the most wanted bandits of the day. Once Belle had a special visitor. He was a cold, silent man with incredible, flickering blue eyes and a straggly dark beard. She told Sam he was a friend from Missouri and he needed a bed for a few days. Sam was suspicious. She seemed to treat the stranger with respect, an odd thing for Belle. He never took off his guns, even when he slept. He left as silently as he had come and many people said that Sam never knew that his house guest had been Jesse James.

Belle was charged four times with horse stealing but was only imprisoned once. That was in 1883 when she became the first female ever to appear for a major crime in front of Hanging Judge Parker. He managed to make the charge stick and sentenced her to six months in the Federal Prison in Detroit. Sam was given one year.

They served their time and returned together to Younger's Bend. After about a year Sam disappeared and Belle was seen hanging on the arm of a criminal type called John Middleton, wanted for murder in Texas. Rumour began to spread that Middleton had also done away with Sam Starr so that he could have the pleasure of Belle's company all to himself. Things appeared in a different light however when one day Middleton was found full of bullet holes and Sam reappeared to take up where he had left off.

The pair were soon being featured on US Government posters promising 10,000 dollars in gold coins for information that led to their arrest. They were wanted, the poster stated, for 'robbery, murder, treason and other acts against the peace and dignity of the United States.' In 1886 they were arrested by US Marshals, taken to Fort Worth and brought before the dreaded Judge Parker. But Belle knew a legal trick or two and the Judge had to dismiss them for lack of evidence.

Belle rode out of town laughing. She was totally unrepentant, thoroughly enjoyed the limelight and gave long, indiscreet interviews to local editors. But she wasn't laughing for long.

That Christmas Sam went into town to drink at a local bar, had too much alcohol, got into an argument with a deputy sheriff and in the ensuing gun fight was shot dead.

Belle mourned him but didn't waste much time before finding herself a new lover. His name was Jim July, a Creek Indian with long black hair falling to his shoulders. He was wanted for robbery and hid out at Younger's Bend until Belle persuaded him to turn himself in at Fort Smith. From experience she felt certain there was not enough evidence to convict him. She advised July to plead 'not guilty' and she said she would support him.

On 3 February 1889 the pair set out towards Fort Smith. They stayed the night at a half-way house but the following morning July was seen to go on alone while Belle turned back. Riding Venus alone on the trail she was shot out of the saddle by an unseen gunman. She was found dying in the dust.

The identity of her killer was never established. Someone called Watson who had been seen arguing with her shortly before her death was charged, then cleared. Some said July himself had offered a gunman 200 dollars to kill her because she had decided not to help him. There was even a theory that her own son, Ed Starr, with whom she was said to have had a stormy, incestuous relationship, had done it. She had recently given him a savage thrashing for riding Venus without her permission.

Whoever killed Belle Starr remains a mystery. But when she was buried in the front yard of the cabin at Younger's Bend, her daughter, Pearl had a splendid stone monument erected at the grave to her mother's memory.

The memorial verse read:

> 'Shed not for her the bitter tear
> Nor give the heart to vain regret
> 'Tis but the casket that lies here
> The gem that fills it sparkles yet.'

A more fitting epitaph might have been Belle's own words: 'I regard myself a a woman who has seen much of life'!

Bonnie Parker

She was barely five feet tall with a tiny waist and well manicured hands. She liked good clothes, fast cars and guns. Apart from those closest to her she didn't give a damn for other human beings and when they got in her way, she mowed them down. Her name was Bonnie Parker.

With her partner in crime, Clyde Barrow, she has become as much part of American folklore as the gunfighters of the Wild West and, like them, over the years has gained an aura of spurious glamour.

Laughing and killing she tore through the southern states at the time of the great American depression, when robber barons, gangsters and strikebreakers were all part of the scene. Her partnership with Clyde Barrow was short, but bloody, and she paid the final price in a hail of bullets.

The legends began before she was buried but those who knew her saw her for what she was: a small time crook with a taste for murderous men and no mercy for those who stood between her and money.

There was nothing about her childhood that made her different. She was born in 1911 into a family of devout Texan Baptists. Her father, a hard working brick layer, died when she was only four. Her mother took her to live in Cement City, near Dallas. At 16 she married her childhood sweetheart Roy Thornton. He soon left her – to serve a 99-year-sentence for murder.

She was working as a waitress in a down-town café when she ran into Clyde Barrow in January 1930. She was just 19 and he was 21. He fell immediately for the petite, fair haired girl with provocative red lips and she, sizing up his somewhat effeminate looks and narrow, snake eyes came to the conclusion that he could be interesting. Bored, restless, missing her husband, Bonnie Parker decided that Clyde Barrow was her new man.

She found out very soon after meeting him that he had been in and out of trouble since the cradle and was, in fact, an incurable criminal. The son of a poor Texan farmer, who just scraped a living to keep his eight children, Clyde was in a boys' reformatory before he was 10 and fell into a life of petty thieving. His habits had not improved. Before their relationship could settle down, he was carted off to spend another two years in jail, leaving Bonnie in a fit of rage and frustration.

When he was 'inside' she managed to smuggle a gun to him. He broke out with two other prisoners, only to be recaptured a few days later after an armed robbery at a railway station. This time he was given 14 years but only served a few months. When Texas elected a woman governor, he was one of those released on parole. Nobody had an idea of what mayhem they had just let loose.

When Bonnie saw him again in March 1932 he was on crutches. He had bribed a fellow prisoner to chop off two toes with an axe so that he would not be suitable for hard labour. Bitter and hard, he vowed he would never let himself be caught again. Bonnie agreed to join up with him.

Lying to her mother, who was the one person she really loved, she said she had taken a job demonstrating cosmetics in a Houston department store. In fact she and Clyde had formed the 'Barrow Gang' and were planning to launch their violence on an unsuspecting community.

By April, Bonnie had been picked up for questioning about a stolen car and when she was released three months later, without being charged, the killing had already started. A jeweller in Hillsborough, Texas, had been gunned down for a measly 40 dollars and the Sheriff and deputy Sheriff of the little town of Atoka in Oklahoma, had also been shot dead. Bonnie climbed onto the bandwagon and they set off on a hell raising tour of Michigan, Kansas and Missouri.

Clyde Barrow had a passion for guns. They accumulated a formidable array of fire arms with which Bonnie liked to pose for photographs. She never hesitated to use any of them. Small town banks, cafés and filling stations were their main target. He had a quick temper and a streak of sadism. Killing people made him laugh.

At first when they had a run of good luck they stayed in decent hotels, ate at fancy restaurants and bought themselves smart clothes. Both were fussy and immaculate in their dress. Bonnie regularly took her clothes and his to a laundry in the country and went to beauty parlours to have her nails painted. She liked the soft life and wished she could have more of it. But the biggest snatch they ever made was 1,400 dollars and, in spite of all the blood they shed, their grand total one month was 76 dollars.

Their exploits made headlines everywhere and they revelled in the publicity. She had been named 'Suicide Sal' and he was 'The Texas Rattlesnake'. But fame meant no more hotels. They travelled constantly sleeping in the cars they had stolen or in empty houses or tourist camps, living off a diet of peanut butter sandwiches and ice cream.

They had been joined by William Daniel Jones, a gas station attendant who had grown up with Clyde and hero worshipped him. He is said to have become Bonnie's lover for she had a voracious appetite for sex which Clyde, with his latent homosexual tendencies, could not satisfy. Jones proved himself a worthy acolyte. While the three of them were trying to steal a car in Temple, Texas, he shot dead the owner's son. Later, when Bonnie and Clyde walked into a trap at Dallas, set for another bank robber, he shot and killed the deputy sheriff.

The robbing and killing went on non-stop. If anyone stood in their way or pursued them, they were shot. By now there were two more additions to the gang: Clyde's brother, Buck and his wife, Blanche. From the time they joined, things began to go wrong.

In March 1933 they all rented an apartment in Joplin, Missouri. It was a mistake. The neighbourhood was respectable and anything unusual did not go unnoticed. One resident reported to the police that he had seen a great deal of coming and going from there and that the occupants scurried in and out like frightened animals. The police sent two squad cars on a routine investigation which ended in a desperate shoot up. They all escaped, leaving two policemen dead on the pavement and another badly wounded.

Unable to rent any more apartments, they had to sleep in their stolen cars. One day Bonnie, always a realist, said 'It can't be long before they get us now. I want to see my mother before I die.' A secret rendezvous was arranged.

Strangely enough, Clyde himself nearly killed Bonnie shortly after. One day, driving in his usual mad fashion, he failed to notice a sign warning that the bridge over a gorge near Wellington, Texas, had collapsed. He approached at 70 mph and plunged over a precipice, turning over twice in mid-air. He was thrown clear but Bonnie had been pinned underneath the wreckage. It caught fire. She pleaded with him to shoot her if he couldn't pull her clear. But a farmer and one of his hands had seen the accident and ran to help release her. She was badly burned and the farmer offered to let her stay and rest while he phoned a doctor. At the mention of a doctor they began to behave very strangely, arousing the farmer's suspicions. He phoned the police. Clyde threatened him with a gun, took his car and escaped with only seconds to spare.

Bonnie was delirious and unless she had medical attention was sure to die. For once in his life, Clyde was frightened. He contacted Buck and his wife and

Bonnie Parker

told them to book a double cabin on a tourist site near Fort Smith, Arkansas. Clyde told everybody she had been injured in an oil stove explosion while they were camping. She refused to go anywhere near a hospital and a doctor and nurse had to be brought in to look after her. The gang robbed another bank to pay the bills, shooting dead a newly elected marshall and, as usual, making their escape in a stolen car.

Again, they were on the run. To give Bonnie a decent night's rest the four of them booked two cabins at a tourist camp near Platte City, Missouri. They kept their curtains drawn all the time which roused suspicion among the other campers. They had to shoot their way out when police arrived in drove and this time they didn't get away scot free. Buck was shot three times in the head and Blanche was temporarily blinded by shattered glass. With Bonnie still in agony from her burns, Buck half dead and Blanche needing a doctor for her eyes, they were in a sorry mess. They hid out in some thick woods near the river at Dexter, Iowa, and Bonnie sent Jones to fetch five chicken dinners from a nearby take-away. The police followed him back. In the bedlam that followed Bonnie managed to get away across the river with Clyde and Jones following but Buck was shot again and was taken to hospital to die. Blanche who had stayed by his side, was clapped in jail to await trial.

After that, because of Bonnie's presentiment that time was running out, they went back to Texas, sleeping in stolen cars and meeting their families in secret. It was Bonnie's idea that Clyde should dress up as a woman in blonde wig. The police, she reasoned, were looking for a man and a woman not for two blondes. The ruse worked.

Recovered from her burns, Bonnie drove the getaway car when they organized a prison break at the beginning of 1934. They got out a man called Ray Hamilton, shot dead a warder and allowed four other prisoners to escape. A few weeks later they machine gunned two highway patrolmen in Grapevine, near Dallas.

They were as nervous as cats and knew they had reached the point of no return. They had killed at least 18 people in their merciless capers. Now the police of Texas, Oklahoma, Louisiana, Arkansas and Kansas were determined to put an end to it.

On the morning of 23 May 1934 Texas Ranger, Frank Hamer, received a tip-off from one of Clyde Barrow's so-called friends. Six police officers in plain dress, waited in bushes by the side of the road just outside Gibsland, Louisiana. Shortly after nine a Ford V-8 Sedan appeared on the dusty, white road. As it drew nearer they could see Bonnie Parker laughing and munching a sandwich. Suddenly guns were rattling out death and the two of them lay sprawled in a river of blood.

They were taken home to Dallas for burial and the crowds were so great that members of their families could hardly get to the graveside. People snatched flowers to take home as souvenirs. Bonnie had written her own epitaph:

> 'Some day they will go down together
> And they will bury them side by side.
> To a few it means grief
> To the law its relief
> But its death to Bonnie and Clyde.'

Madame Rachel

Like a black satin spider Madame Rachel sat in her exotic Bond Street beauty parlour waiting for vain little society flies to become her victims. She lured them in with the promise of everlasting youth and the opportunity of purchasing her fabulous preparations. Miracles, she assured them, could be performed with her royal Arabian soaps, her luxurious Circassian baths, her peach bloom lotions and alabaster creams. Wrinkles and other tiny signs of age could be banished for ever with her greatest discovery of all – magnetic rock water dew from the sands of the Sahara.

Unfortunately many gullible women in the 1860's found Madame Rachel's advertisements for her famous beauty salon quite irresistible. What they did not know until they were trapped in her web was that the lotions and creams were a cover for a far more lucrative profession. Once Madame had chosen her victims she proceeded to strip them of their money and their reputations and to blackmail them with great cunning.

Many dared not tell their husbands how foolish they had been until it was too late. Fear of scandal, even when there was no truth in the allegations, was like a disease in Victorian England. It was a brave man who eventually exposed the truth and wrought Madame to her deserved end. Not, though, until she had brought havoc in some quarters of London society.

Typical of her method was that used on a woman of wealth and position who had been wheedled into taking a course of baths under Madame's personal supervision. One day this lady removed some diamond ear-rings and valuable rings she was wearing and slipped them into a drawer in the dressing room before stepping into the Circassian waters. On her return she found her jewels had gone. She rang the bell and told Madame Rachel of her loss. The old virago fell into a towering rage and declared she did not believe the lady had any jewellery with her. When she persisted Madame ranted: 'It's no use giving yourself airs here. I have had you watched. I know where you live. How would you like your husband to know the real reason for your coming here? What if I tell him about the man who has visited you. . . .' The wretched woman crept home in despair. Though there was not a word of truth in the allegations she did not dare tell her husband the story until after Madame had been arrested.

Sarah Rachel Russell was born into a Jewish theatrical family about the year 1806. Though in her later years she was said to resemble a somewhat dissipated Queen Victoria, in her youth she was good looking with a magnificent head of hair. She was first married to an assistant chemist in Manchester, then to a Mr Jacob Moses who went down with the wreck of the Royal Charter off Anglesey in 1859 leaving her a young family to provide for, and finally to a Mr Philip Leverson who gave her more children but removed himself from the scene by the time she was operating in Bond Street.

In her early days she was a clothes dealer and used to be allowed to take her goods back stage at the London theatres. But she added procuring to her business activities and was thrown out of Drury Lane for making an insulting proposition to one of the dancers, who threw a pot of ale in her face.

Soon after marrying Leverson she fell desperately ill with an unspecified fever. She was taken to King's College Hospital where her head was shaved and she lost every bit of her beautiful and abundant hair. Her distress was so acute that the doctor treating her gave her some lotion to rub on her scalp which, he promised, would produce an even finer crop of hair than she had before. To her amazement his promise came true and she begged him to give her a copy of the prescription. He did so gladly. That prescription was probably the scientific basis of all the lotions and creams which she later described as 'the purest and most fragrant productions of the East!'

By 1860 she was ready to launch out with her new skills. She opened a shop in Bond Street for the sale of cosmetics and other toilet requisites but the venture was a flop and she found herself in the Insolvency Court and later the debtors' prison. Nevertheless she knew she was on to something good and determined to try again, this time using her genius for self publicity and her florid imagination.

Her new premises under the name Madame Rachel were in New Bond Street where she was assisted by her clever young daughters Rachel and Leontie. Madame herself could not even write her name but if she provided the ideas, her daughters could present them.

THIEVES AND OUTLAWS

The new business was launched with a pamphlet entitled *Beautiful for Ever*. It was snapped up by every woman in London who cared about her looks and had money to spend. Its language was wildly romantic and idiotically far-fetched but it worked. Madame claimed to be the sole possessor of the delicate and costly arts whereby the appearance of youth could be produced in the face and figure of an older woman. The secret? Her magnetic rock dew water of the Sahara at two guineas a bottle. She gave her customers an insight into how this magic liquid was obtained: collected in the early morning it was carried from the Sahara to Morocco on swift dromedaries there to be used exclusively by the ladies of the court. She had gained the sole right of importation from the Sultan of Morocco himself 'at an enormous outlay'. As it was guaranteed to 'increase the vital energies, restore the colour to grey hair and remove wrinkles, defects and blemishes' it sold like a bomb.

She offered her customers about 60 preparations including her own special brand of face powder. One shade was called 'Rachel' and brunettes still buy powder of that name in the shops today to suit their darker skins. Her most expensive treatment was the *Complete Royal Arabian Toilet of Beauty* which, she claimed, she had planned for the Sultana of Turkey with marvellous results. She did not say how much the Sultana paid but she charged ordinary mortals around 200 guineas.

However, word had begun to spread that beauty treatment was not all that Madame had to offer at her Bond Street establishment. Business flourished and soon she had enough money to take and furnish an elegant house in Maddox Street and to reserve a box at the Opera, which cost £400 for the season. Creams and lotions did not pay for such luxuries. Procuring, fraud and blackmail did.

Sometimes she played for the highest stakes. At others she would risk everything for a relatively small sum. One day the wife of an admiral called at her salon to buy perfume. Madame, singularly plausible, persuaded her to call again, then again. Each time the Admiral's wife bought a few small items. Eventually she received an exorbitant bill. She managed to pay but stopped calling in at Bond Street. Madame did not intend to let her escape so easily. She sent a bill for £1,000 to the Admiral, claiming she had cured his wife of an upleasant skin affliction. Protests only brought further demands and a threat that unless the bill was settled promptly details of a scandal concerning his wife would be spread throughout London. Fortunately the Admiral went straight to his lawyers and refused to pay a penny. Madame dropped the claim.

The victim who eventually turned on Madame Rachel was a weak, vain little woman of almost unbelieveable gullibility, called Mary Tucker Borradaile. The widow of an Indian army colonel she lived alone in London

85

on her military pension and the modest interest on her investments. She wa
thought to be about fifty though she refused to reveal her age even in cour
She had an almost morbid desire to cling to the pretence of youth and by th
autumn of 1864 it seemed she had found the answer to all her problems. Sh
read an advertisement for Madame Rachel's fabulous oriental treatments fo
enhancing youth, beauty and grace and decided to consult her at all costs.

Madame looked at her new customer with satisfaction. She was 'a skeleto
apparently encased in plaster of Paris, painted pink and white an
surmounted by a juvenile wig'. Her voice was childish and affected, her lac
of brains sadly evident. Madame smiled sweetly and assured her of complet
and lasting rejuvenation.

On her first visit Mrs Borradaile spent a modest £10 though in the twelv
months following her treatment added up to £170 and she paid out othe
sums of money for cosmetics. By the Spring of 1866 it was obvious that despit
all the baths, creams and lotions Mrs Borradaile looked pretty much th
same. Disappointed and peeved she told Madame she had expected to see
better result for her money.

Madame decided she had better move on to the second part of her pla
She informed Mrs Borradaile that a nobleman, Lord Ranelagh, had seen an
fallen in love with her. A few days after this extraordinary announcemer
when they were both sitting in Madame's parlour a tall, elegant man cam
into the shop. Madame addressed him as Lord Ranelagh. 'Are you *really* Lor
Ranelagh?' asked the bemused widow. He bowed, presented her with his car
and left. On several occasions after that she saw his Lordship in the shop an
once he bowed to her.

His Lordship, it appeared, had first seen her in the days of her beauty whe
her husband was still alive, and her impression had been imprinted on h
heart, only to be revived when he saw her again in Madame's parlour. H
begged her to allow Madame to proceed with her 'Beautiful Foreve
programme. This meant an immediate outlay of £1,000 to which the wido
at first objected but seeing that she could not be brought to the pinnacle
perfection required by her suitor for less, the silly woman agreed to foot th
bill.

Madame now began to bring her letters from Lord Ranelagh, which sh
explained, would be signed 'William' for the sake of discretion. All the
courting would be done by letter and they were eventually to be married b
proxy. If Mrs Borradaile began to have her doubts they were no doul
calmed when she received a tender note decorated with Lord Ranelagh
crest and monogram accompanied by a little perfume box and pencil ca
which had apparantly belonged to his 'sainted mother'.

His Lordship had requested his beloved to deliver up to Madame all he jewels as they were not worthy of her future rank. More costly pieces would of course be provided by him in the future. Meanwhile he advised her to buy a few diamonds for their wedding. A coronet and a necklace were ordered from a New Bond Street jeweller for £1,260 and as the widow hadn't got that much in cash she sold some property in Streatham to pay for them. The money was handed to Madame Rachel, never to be seen again. Nor did she see the diamonds. Lord Ranelagh, it seems had needed the cash for some project he had in mind and had suggested that a coronet which had belonged to his mother might be altered for her.

The letters which Lord Ranelagh continued to send to his future wife were extremely coy but included phrases like: 'My own sweet love I am worried to death about money matters. . . .' He claimed he had tried to see her, referring to Madame in a conspiratorial way as 'Granny'. It was obvious, from the letters, that his Lordship was most anxious to preserve an amiable relationship between his fiancée and 'Granny'. If she once jibbed at the demands made on her purse he was quick to reply: 'My own darling Mary, why don't you do as Granny tells you. . . .'

Even the bride to be could not help but notice that sometimes the letters appeared to be written in a different hand. Often there were spelling mistakes and grammatical errors she did not expect from such an aristocratic fiancé. Once the writer inexplicably signed himself 'Edward'. Madame hastily assured her that Lord Ranelagh had not lost his memory but had injured his arm and had had to ask a friend to write the letter for him.

As the wedding day approached it was suggested that she should visit a coach builders in New Bond Street to select a carriage for herself and also a quantity of silver and plate. All her own things, even rings, brooches and trinkets had been packed away by Madame Rachel – they were not considered suitable for her future station in life.

Finally, having stripped the poor creature of everything she owned apart from the clothes she stood up in Madame dealt the final blow. She had her arrested for debt and taken to Whitecross Street prison where she could only obtain her release by making over to her 'creditor' her pension of £350 per annum.

That, according to Madame's calculations, should have been the end of the affair. But the worm turned. Poor, brainless Mary Borradaile wanted revenge. She made contact with her brother-in-law, a Mr Cope, and he came to her rescue. Having obtained her release he instituted proceedings against the woman who had ruined her.

On 20 August 1868 the case of the Queen v Leverson came before the Central Criminal Court in London and provided entertainment for days as the whole ludicrous story spilled out. There were in fact two trials, the jury at the first having failed to agree. Mary Borradaile, it had to be admitted, was hardly a credible witness, tottering into the box with her yellow wig awry and giving her evidence in a childish, lisping voice while Madame, resplendent in black satin and ostrich plumes, watched her through narrowed eyes. Even *The Times* called her a 'self confessed idiot'. But by the time the second trial started on 22 September, Mrs Borradaile had got her spirits up and at one point, when she was being cross examined by Mr Digby, Seymour cried out: 'She's a vile and wicked woman and you are bad too!'

Madame Rachel, accused of obtaining money by false pretences, claimed in her defence that her client was in fact having an affair with a man called William, that she had concocted the story of her engagement to Lord Ranelagh herself and that all her money had been squandered on her real lover. She had merely been a go-between and had helped Mrs Borradaile to deceive her relations out of the kindness of her heart.

There was a great stir when Lord Ranelagh entered the box. He said he recalled meeting the lady in question on two occasions. He had been introduced to her by Madame but had never had the slightest intention of marrying her and had never corresponded with her in any way. He was extremely embarrassed.

Mr Digby Seymour, summing up for the accused, failed to convince the jury that the pathetic widow was the loose conniving woman he would have them believe. The appearance in the witness box of Madame Rachel's two daughters did nothing to help her. In spite of their charm and good looks it soon became obvious that they were lying for all they were worth and the court came to the conclusion that the younger of the two had in fact written the 'William' letters.

The jury was only out for 15 minutes before returning a unanimous verdict of 'Guilty' sending Sarah Rachel Leverson to prison for five years. She was, said one counsel, 'a most filthy and dangerous moral pest.'

Madame served her time in jail then emerged, apparently undaunted, to start up business again as 'Arabian perfumer to the Queen'! No longer welcome in exclusive Bond Street she established herself in a shop at 153, Great Portland Street where she was soon up to her old game. Her sign caught the eye of a young woman called Cecilia Maria Pearce, wife of a Pimlico stockbroker, who though she was only 23 was dissatisfied with her complexion. Before long the old rogue had her deeply involved. This time, however, she had not taken on a fool but a bright young woman who soon realized she was in trouble and consulted her eminent solicitor, Sir George Lewis. For the third time a warrant was issued for Madame Rachel's arrest. She was tried at the Old Bailey in April 1878 and sentenced to five years imprisonment, the judge regretting he could not give her more. But Madame did not serve out her term. She died in Woking jail on 12 October 1880.

Perhaps the evidence given by Sabina Pilley, one of her assistants, finished her off. For Sabina had torn aside the veil of mystery and divulged her exotic secrets. The fabulous Arabian complexion treatment, for instance, consisted of starch, fuller's earth, pearl ash and water with a dash of hydrochloric acid. As for the Royal Arabian and Circassian baths, so much enjoyed by the Sultana of Turkey. Alas, they were just hot water and bran.

Chapter Four

Ruthless Rulers

There have been many great women controlling
the destinies of people. There have also been some
bloodthirsty tyrants. Sometimes the two have gone
together. Greatness has not excluded tyranny and
vice versa. But feminine passion mixed with
politics can have a diabolical effect....

Livia

ivia was one of the most cruelly ambitious women the world has ever
known. Her portrait was painted with fine precision by Robert Graves
in his book '*I, Claudius*' as the she-wolf of all the Roman Empresses.

She was the wife of the great Caesar Augustus, who owed at least some of
his glory to her, but her passion for personal power led her to such acts of
treachery that she stands alone.

Her family was one of the most illustrious in Rome and her ancestral stock
more ancient than Rome itself. She had a high bred kind of beauty and a
disdainful air that came naturally to her. Her mind ranked as one of the finest
but when she chose to she could ensnare men with her seductive manner.

When she was at the height of her beauty and married to Tiberius Nero,
Augustus became intrigued by her. Caesar was then in his prime, a splendid
looking man with fair, tightly curled hair, a typical Roman nose and
sparkling eyes. He was also blessed with an affable temperament, except when
at war when he was as cruel as any. He found Livia, with her satin smooth
charm, vastly different from his wife, the odd and gloomy Scribonia.

Livia could not have left Augustus in doubt for long about her own feelings
for she was soon pregnant and general gossip assumed the child to be his.
Unfortunately Tiberius Nero was an old enemy and could not be bought. So,
taking the bull by the horns, Augustus asked Tiberius to give him his wife and
left him in no doubt as to what would happen if he refused. It did not take the
lady long to assess who would further her ambitions better.

Augustus consulted the oracles pretending to be anxious about whether he
might marry a woman already with child. The oracles were favourable, so the
wedding took place. Tiberius was asked to give her away and, perhaps to
soothe his ruffled ego, was guest of honour at the great feast that followed.

Three months later Livia had a son who was named Drusus. Augustus sent
the baby to be brought up by Tiberius in case it should be thought his own,
but ribald jokes about who was really the father caused a great deal of
laughter among the ordinary people.

Two historic battles soon separated the Emperor of Rome and his new
Empress. In the first he defeated the great Roman general, Pompey, in one of
the bloodiest battles known at that time. He went on to bring an end to Mark
Anthony at the famous battle of Actium, after which Cleopatra took the asp
and killed herself rather than be taken back to Rome in triumph.

Augustus returned home to be loaded with honour and glory and Livia basked luxuriously in its reflection. A town called Liviada was built in her honour. She was given the most pompous titles, poets celebrated her in verse and temples were erected in her name.

Victory meant a time of peace. In Rome Augustus anticipated all her wishes so that in time her authority was as absolute as his own. She always showed great tenderness towards him, but there was also a great deal of art and cunning in her behaviour, which he did not find out until it was too late. She took care at that stage that nobody should have anything to reproach her with. One day, some young men, sporting about, had appeared before her stark naked. They were condemned to death but she had them pardoned saying that a naked man made no more impression on the imagination of a virtuous woman than a statue.

Her two sons, Tiberius by her former husband, and Drusus, grew to be men. She saw to it that they were given important status in the Roman army and that their victories, however trivial, were treated as triumphs. Tiberius was cruel and arrogant and addicted to debauchery of the worst kind. Augustus gave his opinion that if he ever came to power he would cause the greatest misery and suffering. Drusus, on the other hand, was such a fine man that the Emperor would have liked to have named him as his successor but felt it would confirm peoples' suspicions that he was his own son.

As it was he chose his nephew and son-in-law, Prince Marcellus as heir presumptive, a soldier he considered to have noble qualities. This was not what Livia had in mind. Her one aim now was to pave the way to the throne for her son, Tiberius. Soon after Augustus had made his announcement, Prince Marcellus died in great agony. Livia had struck her first blow.

As if in answer, fate threw a tragedy across her path. Her son Drusus was killed on his way back to Rome after a battle. Her grief was so great that philosophers were sent for to give her what comfort they could. From then on she became more deadly and doubled her efforts for Tiberius. With Prince Marcellus out of the way she thought matters could be arranged quite easily for she had advised Augustus so skilfully in other matters that he began to think her always right. But then he took the step of marrying his daughter, Julia, widow of Prince Marcellus, to Agrippa. She gave birth to two sons, Gaius and Lucius, both in direct line to the throne. For a time there was nothing Livia could do.

But as the years passed and Augustus grew older she determined afresh to get rid of any obstacle that stood between her son and the throne. She made her plans without any outward show of treachery or violence, like a snake creeping up in the night. By now the Emperor was completely under her domination and her word had become, if anything, more respected in Rome than his. People did not dare disobey her.

The day came when the two young princes Gaius and Lucius met sudden and tragic ends, the first in Lycia as he was returning from war, the second in Marseilles. People were aghast at the awfulness of the tragedy and Augustus could not be comforted. Feeling that soon he would have no kin of his own left in the world, he adopted his daughter's youngest son, Agrippa, together with Tiberius. This step divided the Empire between his own grandson and Livia's son. He thought she would be pleased, but she was furious that all her well laid plans had ended in this. Agrippa had to be got rid of but another death, so soon, would not be satisfactory. She set to work to poison the Emperor's mind with malicious talk and rumours about his grandson, none of which were true. But Augustus, believing her implicitly, wept and had him banished to the island of Planasia. To all Rome the punishment seemed unjust and cruel. Agrippa had not the polished style of the other princes, but as far as anyone knew, this was his only crime.

Augustus often complained of his cruel destiny in losing one by one so many members of his family. He began to think back on all that had happened and suddenly longed to see Agrippa, the grandson he had exiled. He made up his mind to go to his island prison. He kept his visit a secret from anyone, even Livia, for perhaps at last he was beginning to have suspicions. Only his friend Fabius Maximus knew. But this man told his wife and his wife told Livia. This produced such venom, such anger, that Caesar should have acted without her knowledge, that she made the most terrible decision of all to kill Augustus and his grandson.

Even with her smooth tongue she could not conceal her true feelings on his return, when she told him there was 'no occasion for all this secrecy.' One day at his palace in Nola, lying in the very room where his father, Octavius, had died, she brought him a dish of figs. He ate them with pleasure, but they were full of poison. As he died, Augustus spoke to Livia with words of tenderness, but those close enough thought they saw a light of dawning horror in his eyes.

His death was kept secret for some time because Tiberius was absent. Livia fretted and paced her palace floors willing her son to come home. As soon as he arrived, the death of Augustus and the succession of Tiberius were announced simultaneously. Poor Agrippa was murdered. Livia said that Augustus had ordered it in his will but everyone knew this was just another of her crimes.

The Romans, by now afraid of this she-wolf, lavished fresh honours and titles upon her. This was just what she had schemed for. Now, the glory of being mother of the Emperor would give her even greater stature. But she had not reckoned with Tiberius. She had bred a son worthy of her.

He was jealous of her honours, looking upon them as diminishing his own stature. He gave orders that her household was not to be increased by a singl

Livia

officer. He was in fact indifferent to her. She irritated him by constantly reminding him that he owed his throne to her.

This ingratitude did not stop her. She took every step necessary to ensure that he should reign without trouble or threat. She persecuted all those of Augustus's family she had still left alive. However, there was still Prince Germanicus, her own grandson, who, like his father, Drusus, was brave and honest. Tiberius himself was jealous of his fame, hated hearing of his triumphs and resented his victories. Orders were sent to Syria where he was in charge of the army and he was killed by poison.

Mother and son grew further apart. Tiberius hated Livia's boundless ambition. The pomp and magnificence with which she surrounded herself were anathma to him. He was just in time to stop her putting her name before that of Augustus on a memorial dedicated to the great Caesar.

Finally, to escape her, he left Rome and went to Capri where he spent the rest of his life indulging his taste for nameless debauchery. Livia reigned absolute in his place. She enjoyed herself and lived until she was 80. When news of her end was carried to Tiberius in Capri he said he could not go to Rome. He excused himself with weak stories of ill health and other difficulties, but it was thought he dared not let it be seen how terribly his appalling life had aged him.

Livia was placed in a mausoleum with Augustus, and her grandson, Caligula, pronounced her funeral oration. The senate wanted to make her a goddess, but Tiberius, in a fit of retaliation would not allow it. He said he did not think she would want such a thing. At that, she must have stirred in her grave.

Catherine the Great

'She is romantic, ardent and passionate. She has a bright glassy hypnotic look like that of a wild animal. She has a big forehead and unless I am mistaken, a long and terrifying future marked upon it. She is thoughtful and friendly and yet when she approaches me I automatically back away. She frightens me.'

So wrote the Chevalier D'Eon, secret agent and wily observer at the Russian Court in 1756. The woman he was writing about became Catherine the Great, Empress of Russia and, to this day, one of the most remarkable women ever to sit on a throne.

D'Eon summed up her complexity. She was no tyrant, yet she demanded blind obedience. She thought only of making Russia great, yet treated the wretched serfs as scarcely human. She could never be directly accused of murder, yet the assassinations of Tzar Ivan VI and her husband, Peter III, undoubtedly left blood on her hands. She remained a virgin until she was 23, then for the rest of her life hardly ever went to bed without a lover.

Strangely enough, Catherine had not a drop of Russian blood in her veins. She was German.

Her given name was Sophie Augusta Frederica of Anhalt-Zerbst and she was born at Stettin, Pomerania, in April 1729. Her father was Prince Christian Augustus, an impoverished royal who had been given the post of Commandant at Stettin. Her mother, related to the great ducal house of Holstein, was a discontented woman who considered she was living a dull, provincial life, unworthy of her status and talents. She had no real affection for her daughter. But in spite of her father's lack of money and her mother, Princess Johanna's coldness, the young Sophie had a normal childhood.

Life changed dramatically when she reached the age of 15. Mysterious comings and goings, letters with imperial seals and her mother's excitement were all for one reason. She had been chosen as a possible bride for the Grand Duke Peter of Russia. Frederick of Prussia had probably suggested her because her humble place in the list of German princesses was thought more likely to make her grateful for the honour and therefore, easy to manipulate.

Summoned to the Russian Imperial Court by the Empress Elizabeth, mother and daughter set off with a scarcely adequate wardrobe, the Prince refusing to spend money on fancy clothes. They were received with great splendour. Princess Sophie nearly fainted when the Empress aproached her, looking like a goddess in silver watered silk and diamonds. This beautiful, imposing woman known only too well for her vanity and cruelty, examined her coolly and liked what she saw. Princess Sophie, with her beautiful pale skin, long dark hair, blue eyes and natural grace could be the right choice. After days of further scrutiny, during which she felt like a piece of merchandise, she was accepted as the Grand Duke's bride.

When she first saw him, she was appalled. Twisted and deformed with an ugly, thick lipped face, he behaved like a whimpering child one minute and a drunken sadist the next. But what mattered was her destiny. She took the name Catherine on 28 June 1744, the day of her conversion to the Orthodox faith and the following day became engaged. The Grand Duke was not much older than her. They sometimes found enough in common to keep each other company and play games in the palace corridors. But as the days went by a growing mutual dislike became obvious. It was decided to bring forward the day of the wedding.

They were married in Byzantine splendour, both dressed in cloth of silver and smothered in jewels. That night, after a great dinner and ball, he fell into bed brutishly drunk. Catherine did not know whether to be angry or relieved. On following nights he often took his toy soldiers to bed and played with them on the counterpane. It was obvious to everyone that the marriage was a failure.

The Grand Duke, pitifully aware of his own ugliness, took a perverse pleasure in rousing Catherine's disgust. He was impotent by night and repulsive by day; terrified of the Empress and irritated by his wife's devotion to her duties. She had almost made herself ill by spending long hours learning the Russian language and Orthodox rites.

After eight years of marriage, Catherine was still a virgin. She was desperate for love. One day she decided to flirt with one of the chamberlains at her Court whose name she discovered was Serge Saltykov. He was attractive to women and knew it. Although married to one of the Empress's ladies-in-waiting he had travelled and learned sophisticated manners and habits. Catherine, whose appetite for beautiful young men became a mania, was bowled over. Before long they were lovers. Nobody seemed to mind. The Grand Duke had his whores and the Empress turned a blind eye for state reasons. There was still no heir.

In 1754 Catherine became pregnant and when she gave birth to a baby son he was called the Grand Duke Paul. Saltykov was advised to travel for the sake of his health and the Empress whisked the child away to bring him up herself. Catherine was heartbroken, but made up her mind never to be hurt by a man again. When she returned to court, the steel in her nature had begun to show.

'My misfortune is that my heart cannot be happy even for an hour without love' she was to write later. Fortunately for her there now appeared a romantic young Pole, Count Stanislas Poniatowsky. He was not as handsome as Saltykov but had a cultivated mind and great sensitivity. Catherine yearned for him. Once she fixed her eyes on a man, he was as good as lost. Though nervous at first, Poniatowsky agreed to disguise himself as a tailor or musician to gain access to the Grand Duchess' apartment. He was caught slipping out one morning and dragged before the Grand Duke. 'Confide in me,' said Peter smoothly, 'and it can all be arranged.' He was indifferent to his wife's amours, but liked to know what was going on. It was a dangerous moment. The Grand Duke was terrifyingly unpredictable and could have run him through with a sword. As it turned out, Peter fetched his mistress and the four of them played a game of cards.

Poniatowsky became a pawn in an intricate game of diplomacy that was being played in St Petersburg and in the end he was driven from Russia.

Years later Catherine broke his spirit by a callous political manoeuvre, making him King of Poland one day and forcing him to abdicate the next. The humiliation killed him.

Swift on the heels of the Pole came one of the most important and useful men in her life.

Gregory Orlov was a magnificent Tartar, one of five brothers, all noted for their looks and their strength. He was only moderately intelligent and had no deep conversation to offer her, but he had marvellous sensuality and made her feel alive. Politically he was a brilliant choice. The whole Orlov clan was proud of having one of themselves chosen to be the Grand Duchess' lover and they vowed undying life-long loyalty, raising support among their fellow officers. Having the army behind her was to be vitally important.

On Christmas Day 1761 the Empress Elizabeth died and suddenly the ugly, debauched nephew she had terrorised was Peter III, Tzar of all the Russians. He went wild with his newly attained power. He mocked Elizabeth's coffin, refused to wear mourning and played the fool in her funeral procession. Catherine, to give a good impression, wore black from head to foot and kept vigil by the embalmed body of the woman she had hated.

Once again she was pregnant, this time by Orlov. When her baby son was born, he was sent out to foster parents. Peter, who had made threats to crush the wife who was ice cold to him, shouted across the table at a banquet: 'God knows where she gets her children from, but at least I know they are not mine!'

That sealed his fate. From that time on Catherine began to scheme against him and to await his downfall. He dug his own grave. Mad with power he made enemies on every side, mocking the Orthodox religion and courting his great Hero, Frederick the Great, who had beaten Russia to her knees.

The coup d'etat which made Catherine the ruling Empress came so swiftly that people scarcely had time to realize what had happened. It took place dramatically, by night, with the Orlov brothers predominant and the army solidly behind her. Next day, Sunday 30 June 1762 she made a triumphal entry into St Petersburg, with all the bells ringing.

It had been bloodless and swift. She took power at the head of 20,000 soldiers, dressed in officer's uniform, and all the important factions submitted to her.

Peter, green with fear and whimpering like a child had been bundled off his throne and into a carriage to be imprisoned in the fortress of Schlusselburg, a place long associated with torture and misery and which he dreaded. He pleaded with Catherine to let him keep his mistress, his dog, his negro and his violin. She wrote sardonically 'Fearing scandal, I only granted him the last

Catherine the Great

three.' There was nothing but hatred left in their feelings for each other.

Only three weeks after he had been deposed, Peter was dead. Catherine always maintained he had died from apoplexy, but this was not true. It was known that he did not die of natural causes but from violence. The full story of his death has never been told but at the time it was universally believed that he had been poisoned by a glass of burgundy then, when that did not work fast enough, strangled with a table napkin by one of the Orlov brothers. Catherine swore she had nothing to do with it, but she was not believed. Feeble though he was, as long as he remained alive he had been a threat.

Another threat, infinitely more pathetic, was removed very soon after. Catherine had been to visit a prisoner in his cell. He was a young man of 22 with a thin white face and wild eyes whose mind had slowly atrophied in isolation. He was called Prisoner Number 1 but he was in fact the rightful ruler of Russia, Tzar Ivan VI. Shut away since he was six years old by the Empress Elizabeth, he knew nothing of the world but damp prison walls and iron bars. As Catherine stood before him he mumbled his claims over and over again. The fact that he should have been Emperor was the only thing he could remember. She stared at him with cold eyes, then left.

Her orders were that the guard on him was to be doubled and he was to be killed outright if any attempt was made to rescue him. She knew she had enemies and sure enough certain groups began to talk of restoring the martyr to his rightful place and getting rid of the German woman. One night, Ivan was stabbed to death by a hot-headed lieutenant called Basil Morovitch. But Morovitch had not acted alone and again the rumours started. Was he merely an agent for Catherine?

Only one rival remained – her own son. She loved the Grand Duke Paul in her way but had him brought up to be submissive. After he asked why his 'father' had been killed she made sure he remained a nonentity.

Her whole aim was to raise the power and might of Russia over all other empires and to expand her frontiers as far as possible. She had a rock-like will when it came to achieving her ends. She claimed to hold liberal views but did nothing to change the barbaric, cruel and miserable life endured by the millions of human beings called serfs. She handed them out by the thousand to reward the architects of her coup d'etat. Serfs had no more rights than defenceless animals and were often valued at less. In Catherine's Russia a pedigree dog was worth 2,000 roubles but you could get a male serf for 300 roubles and a young peasant girl cost less than one hundred.

Catherine never forgot what the Orlovs had done for her. Gregory and his brothers, over a period of ten years, received seven million roubles as tokens of her gratitude. This did not include gifts of palaces and jewels. On their estates they were absolute lords of 45,000 serfs.

THE WORLD'S WICKEDEST WOMEN

Gregory Orlov remained her great love and she allowed him to behave with such familiarity that people began to resent his influence on her. He wore a miniature of her, studded with diamonds, as a mark of her special favour and soon became so aware of his power that he was no longer satisfied with his role as lover. He tried to persuade Catherine to marry him so that he could be consort. When he received her refusal with a show of haughty bad temper she began to see that it was time for him to go. She conferred on him the title of Prince then sent him off on his travels. He dazzled Europe with a succession of magnificent uniforms but caused one wit to remark 'He is like an ever boiling pan of water which never cooks anything.' On his return the Empress gave him a marble palace and he presented her with an enormous blue Persian diamond, the 'Nadir-Shah' which became known as the Orlov diamond.

She was glad to see him and put up with his behaviour because he had such a special place in her life. But there was already another lover in her bed, a dark, good looking young man called Vasilchikov. The shock brought him to his senses but it was too late.

Waiting in the wings was the most famous of all Catherine's lovers, the great Prince Potemkin. She was 45 when he stormed her emotions, causing her to write him scorching letters confessing her greed for him. 'Every cell in my body reaches towards you, oh, barbarian! .... Thank you for yesterday's feast.' Yet it was power not love that Potemkin was seeking and it was her mind that he valued. Between kisses they would discuss affairs of state and gradually Catherine began to see that he was more than a lover to her. He was indispensible and worked with her to further her ambition and all the great schemes she had for Russia. When she heard he had died, she fainted.

At a time of life when her ardour should have been on the wane Catherine started on a string of young lovers whose only qualifications were beauty of face and form. She adored young men, even the most humble. The money Catherine lavished on her favourites is almost without parallel. In cash alone, forgetting all the lavish presents and houses she dispensed, she cost Russia one hundred million roubles. Potemkin had 50 million of this sum but at least he gave Russia the Crimea, the Caucasus and the Black Sea!

Potemkin's death was such a terrible blow to Catherine that she never wholly recovered. Her last favourite was a brilliant, handsome courtier called Plato Zubov, who soon began to show a taste for insolence and intrigue. He was forty years her junior, and though she was never to know it, he was to strike the first blow in the murder of her son after he ascended the throne.

Her end came suddenly, as the snow fell on St Petersburg. She suffered a stroke, from which she never recovered and died in her bed on 7 November 1796.

Queen Christina of Sweden

Through the Monaldesco affair the whole world came to know that Christina of Sweden meant what she said when she cried: 'I never forgive'. This strange queen who dressed as a man, despised women, and after abandoning her throne spent a lifetime storming about Europe, shocked even the most worldly by her part in the cold blooded murder.

It took place while she was staying at Fontainbleau in France, an unwelcome and uninvited guest as far as the French government was concerned. With her were two of her Italian courtiers, Count Santinelli, her captain of the guard, and the Marquis Monaldesco, her chief equerry. The two men loathed each other. They were constantly plotting and scheming to see which of them could find greater favour with the queen. Santinelli had cheated and swindled her over her property in Rome and the Marquis, seeking to incriminate him, forged a series of letters in his hand including, for good measure, insinuations about her relationship with a Cardinal in Rome and her ambition to take the throne of Naples.

The whole thing went desperately wrong for Monaldesco. Christina, always in the habit of opening other people's letters, recognized his hand through the forgery and came to the conclusion that it was he who was betraying her. She summoned him to her room and asked him what he would consider a fitting punishment for a traitor. 'Death', said Monaldesco, thinking she was convinced of Santinelli's guilt. 'Good', said the Queen. 'Remember what you have said. For my part, let me tell you, I never forgive.'

The climax to the terrible affair came on 10 November 1657 when the Queen summoned him to the *Galerie de Cerfs* at Fontainbleau. She had also summoned Father Lebel, prior of the nearby Mathurin Monastery and told him to read the letters. Monaldesco had a sudden premonition of what was to happen, but it was too late. The doors were guarded by soldiers and the Queen, dressed in black and toying with an ebony cane talked of trivial matters for a while as though playing for time. Suddenly Santinelli and two guards strode into the room, bared daggers in their hands.

Trembling, Monaldesco threw himself on his knees and begged for her pardon, confessing the forgery was in his hand. He pleaded with her to listen, to let him tell the whole story. She turned to the prior and said 'prepare his soul for death' then left the gallery.

Lebel followed her asking her to have mercy. Serene and unmoved she replied that after the treachery this man had shown towards her he could not have mercy. Even the rogue Santinelli went down on his knees and begged her to change her mind, to let the case come before the Royal Courts. Christina merely urged him to make haste.

Monaldesco died a terrible death. He had put on armour underneath his ordinary clothing and his executioners found it hard to kill him. He took 15 minutes to die and his screams must have reached her ears. She salved her conscience by sending money to the local convent to have prayers said for the repose of his soul.

To her enemies the affair offered proof of what they considered her arrogance and lack of humanity. They thought that far from being executed for political treachery Monaldesco had probably come into possession of some delicate personal secrets which she preferred not to be known.

Queen Christina was an extraordinary woman whose whole life was an enigma. She amazed everybody by her learning, the brilliance of her mind and the vivacity of her conversation. She also worried them by her odd sexuality, her meddling in politics and her lack of feeling for people generally. She always preferred the company of men and was awkward in feminine pursuits. When young she thought nothing of hunting reindeer in snow and biting cold for ten hours at a time, galloping at such a crazy speed that no one could keep up with her. Whenever she could she dressed in men's clothing. Her sexual leanings were not straightforward. Although she fell deeply in love with one of her ladies-in-waiting as a young woman, the other great loves of her life were all men.

Christina gave up the throne of Sweden because she had become bored with the plain, Protestant life and bored with being queen. She also refused to marry. For the rest of her life she went flinging and swaggering about Europe, creating such problems that men went pale when they saw her coming.

When she was born on 8 December 1626 she was so hairy and cried with such a deep voice that everyone told her father, the great King Gustavus Adolphus, that he had a son. The mistake caused great embarrassment but Gustavus was typically good natured about it and said 'The little thing will grow up to be clever. She has already fooled us all.'

He was killed in battle in 1632 when she was six and five regents took over until she reached her majority. They kept her away from her mother's melancholy influence as much as possible. After Gustave's death, Queen Marie lived in a room hung with black in which candles burned night and day. She kept a shroud by her side and Gustave's heart, encased in gold, above her bed. As a result, Christina received a somewhat masculine education, directed almost exclusively by men.

Queen Christina of Sweden

On her 18th birthday she took the oath as King of Sweden as it was not considered suitable to have the first woman to sit upon the throne called merely Queen. For ten years Christina handled politics vigorously and well. Europe was agog at this extraordinary girl whose statesmanship was remarkably mature, whose thirst for knowledge had become a mania and who was so unorthodox. It seemed she only required four hours sleep a night, spent the minumum time on her appearance, preferring Hungarian riding clothes of masculine cut and had declared her love for a woman.

Her great passion was for the beautiful Ebba Sparre, a lady-in-waiting. The girl was already betrothed to the Count Jacob de la Gardie and Christina tried in every way to take her away from him. The Queen's intensity must have frightened her and she had no intention of turning down a splendid offer of marriage to become an old maid. She married the Count while Christina suffered agonies of jealousy. Typically, she never forgave him.

But Christina was never predictable. Just as everyone had made up their minds she was lesbian she took as her favourite the brilliant, French oriented brother of this same Count, and it was obvious she fell deeply in love with him. In the eyes of the world he was her lover but eventually she loaded him with honours and sent him away, perhaps because she was aware of the ambiguity of her sexual nature.

Christina had become bored with Protestant Sweden. She began to regard the teachings of Luther and Calvin as 'moth-eaten' and called her Prime Minister an 'Old Goth'. She wanted to strengthen Sweden's alliance with France, a move which her ministers regarded as a sin against the Protestant cause. She admired French culture and the French way of living and had already enlivened the court with considerable style. She came under the influence of four foreign *bon viveurs* who were only too ready to help her change and life became all festivals and ceremonials, ballets and masquerades. She began to neglect the affairs of state to such an extent that sometimes she would let a month go by without seeing her ministers. What they did not know was that one of her friends, the elegant Spanish Ambassador, Don Antonio Pimentel, had already brought numerous Jesuit priests to Stockholm in disguise and that she was on the verge of conversion.

Christina had two shocks ready for her government. First, she refused to marry. She told them 'Marriage would entail many things to which I cannot become accustomed and I really cannot say when I shall overcome this inhibition. . . .' Then she told them she intended to abdicate and suggested the throne should be offered to her cousin, Prince Charles Gustavus, who would be better able to secure the succession. Their reaction, and that of her people, was as though she had committed high treason. Who would have believed this of the daughter of the great King Gustavus!

She greeted the day of her abdication with relief. There was a rather ludicrous little ceremony in which she had to put on her crown, her blue velvet coronation robe and her insignia then have them stripped from her. No one dared touch the crown and she had to take it off herself. The coronation of Charles x took place the same day.

Seeming to care little for the chaos, anxiety and disappointment she left behind she dressed in male clothes, took the name Count Dohna and set off for Denmark, promising she would return, though she had no intention of doing so. The new King found his palace in Stockholm so emptied of furniture and carpets that he had difficulty finding somewhere to sleep. Christina had shipped them off to Rome, where she intended to bask in the approval of the Pope.

On 23 December 1654 Christina made a triumphal entry into Brussels where she declared herself a Catholic. Those who knew her doubted her motives and thought she made the change because she liked the colour and pageantry. People crowded round to catch a glimpse of her. They saw a woman of medium height dressed in a strange mixture of clothes with a ribbon tied carelessly round her unruly hair. Her face was rather sallow and her features strong, her nose being somewhat aquiline. She rode like a man.

She enjoyed herself in Brussels with one long round of festivities, but her reputation for unconventional behaviour became so widespread that the government in Sweden threatened to stop her income. The scandal sheets accused her of every kind of sexual irregularity. She was called the 'Queen of Sodom'.

The Pope, Alexander VII sent word that he would receive her in Rome just before Christmas in 1655. It was the moment she had been waiting for. Dressed magnificently for once, but riding her horse astride like a man, she made her way towards the Vatican through streets festooned with flowers, triumphal arches and flags. Fanfares and salvos greeted her all the way along the route. Then she walked in a brilliant procession to where the Pope waited to give her the sacrement of confirmation. She was the sensation of Rome.

But if the Pope thought he had gained a model convert he was soon to be disillusioned. She had had her fill of piety and had other things to do. Humility was never one of her virtues and it did not suit her to be openly humble as His Holiness wished. She made fun of the relics and jabbered away to her companions during mass. Being informed of this the Pope sent her a rosary and begged her to tell her beads while in church. She answered bluntly that she had no intention of being a mumbling Catholic.

Worse was to come. She won over two of his cardinals by her brilliant talk. One of them, Cardinal Colonna, became so involved that he fell in love with her and the exasperated Pope had to send him away from Rome to avoid a public scandal. The other was Cardinal Azzolino, whom she undoubtedly loved and who became a devoted friend to her, though no one is sure of the relationship.

Though she made fun of Italian tastes and manners, the intellectuals gathered around her and she pleased them by inaugurating an Academy of Moral Science and Literature. She began to concern herself with politics with the most unfortunate results and Alexander began to wish his guest would go. She too had become tired of being under the eye of Rome.

She decided to leave for a time but was obliged to sell horses, carriages and jewellery to get herself to Paris. It was worth it. The French gave her a state reception watched by 200,000 people. She rode into the city astride her charger wearing a hat trimmed with sable plumes and a tunic heavily trimmed with gold and silver lace. She was escorted by 16,000 men of the Paris militia and 10,000 horses.

People were rather surprised at the coolness with which she accepted this display in her honour. 'Providence arranged that I should be born surrounded on every hand with laurels and palms....' she explained sanctimoniously. 'All Sweden went on its knees and worshipped me in my cradle'. She was not liked by the ladies of the Court but impressed the men by her intellectual brilliance and mastery of languages.

She stayed at Fontainebleau and it was then that the Monaldesco execution took place. The French were appalled at what they described as a medieval barbarity. She had to wait several months for the affair to blow over before she could return to Paris. Cardinal Mazarin, her host, gave her to understand that the sooner she went, the better, and she set out once more for Rome.

Her reception in Rome was very unfriendly. Only the devoted Cardinal Azzolino who had written to her regularly while she was away, seemed delighted to see her. The Pope wanted nothing to do with her and complained to the Venetian Ambassador that she was a barbarian. He neither replied to her letter informing him of her arrival or received her at his summer palace. He was furious with her and suggested she took residence outside Papal See. But he did grant her an annuity and appointed Azzolini to look after her financial affairs.

As the years passed Christina began to be plagued with regrets. She no longer seemed to have any place in the world. Her position was too humble for her liking. It was at about this time she heard that a woman called Gyldener who was the same age as herself and strongly resembled her had been passing herself off as Queen Christina in Sweden. Several months elapsed before her real identity was discovered. Full of rage the exiled Queen sent word to King Charles to have the wretched woman put to death. The

King decided to be more merciful and put her in prison for a month on a diet of bread and water.

Christina now began to meddle in European politics and at one point even suggested a new crusade to unite all Christian countries against the Turks, saying that modern Turkey must be completely destroyed. Nobody took much notice of her.

She seized upon another ambition: to rule another European country so that her name would mean something again in the councils of the world. The throne of Naples was vacant and she wanted to be queen. First, however, she wanted to drive the Spaniards out of Sicily and asked France to help her. But France would not commit herself to Christina in any way.

Then, in February 1660 another throne became empty, the one she had once abdicated so joyfully. Charles x had died suddenly leaving as his heir a five-year-old child. Christina made up her mind to go to Sweden. When she got as far as Hamburg the Swedes sent her a letter more or less asking her to go away, but she ignored it. For one thing she wanted to find out what would happen to the already desperate state of her finances. She also wanted to revive her image as a great queen and possibly spy out the land for the future. In Stockholm she was received with due respect and even given her apartments in the royal palace. But her hosts were wary. They were afraid that she was beginning to regret her abdication and would take this opportunity to make a claim to the throne. They allowed her to retire to one of her estates for a time where she ordered mass to be said regularly, then, after a decent interval the government hinted that it was high time she left.

The remaining years were spent wandering about the world, often dishevelled, and as she grew older any charm she once had disappeared under a layer of fat. Her eyes, too, took on a steely, hard look and she was inclined to make extraordinary statements like 'to attack me is to attack the sun.'

She returned to Rome at last and lived for a while in a villa where the Garibaldi Monument now stands. Her relationship with Cardinal Azzolino had become more and more remote. She swore she would love him to the end but he was in line for the papal crown and had to watch his reputation.

There was one more throne she had her eye on; that of Poland. But the Poles, thinking over her reputation, her life as a man-woman and her material dependence on the Pope, declined her offer. They chose the Duke of Lithuania instead and sternly reminded her of Monaldesco's assassination.

Her last years in Rome were full of cultural activity and she gathered a loyal circle around her. In February 1689 her health began to waver. She contracted a lung disease. The Pope gave her his absolution and promised to visit her in person but before he could do so she died, on 19 April, with Azzolino by her side.

Tzu-hsi – The Dragon Empress

The hatred and cruelty of one woman, Tzu-hsi, Dragon Empress of China, came to a terrifying climax in the celestial city of Peking one hot summer's day in 1900.

At the height of the Boxer rebellion – that great upsurgence of Chinese against foreigners and Christians – the French cathedral was burned to the ground killing hundreds of men, women and children. She watched the blaze from a nearby hill. Her order for a ceasefire in the bombardment came, not from mercy, but because her head ached.

While the red turbaned hooligans she championed rampaged around the city yelling 'Burn, burn, burn, Kill, kill, kill' she was engaged in painting delicate designs of bamboo on silk or arranging exquisite water picnics on the palace lake. While Christians were massacred, thousands of Chinese converts among them, she tended her four-inch-long finger nails, shielded with jade, and tottered round her gardens in jewel-encrusted shoes.

'Let no one escape,' she had ordered 'so that my Empire may be purged. . . .' Her soldiers were offered money for the heads of Europeans. Yet many of those who barricaded themselves in the British Legation and staunchly held out until rescue, remembered taking tea with her and being charmed, especially when she confided that she had a great admiration for Queen Victoria and kept a photograph of her beside her bed.

This extraordinary, complex woman, who controlled the destiny of 400 million people for nearly 50 years, believed herself to be the cleverest woman in the world. But eventually her feudal outlook, her conviction that China was the centre of the world and that all foreigners were barbarians, brought about the end of the great Ch'ing dynasty. Her death in 1908 opened the floodgates to change.

Though she stood only five feet tall her appearance was often dramatised, especially in her youth, by mask like make-up and magnificent garments jewelled and fantastically embroidered in brilliant colours. Her raven black hair was never cut. She took great care of her appearance and her health, eating vast amounts of milk curdled with rennet but only small amounts of other foods, always of the finest quality.

She was the daughter of a minor Manchu mandarin. Born in November 1835 her destiny, according to the structure of the society she lived in, was to become a concubine. She was sent to the Imperial court at the age of 16 and a contemporary description of her, given in Marina Warner's biography of the Dragon Empress, is enchanting. Like all Manchu girls she whitened her face and rouged two spots of high colour on her cheeks. Her bottom lip was painted in a scarlet cherry drop. Sometimes she added blue to her eyelids and outlined her eyes with khol. Above this mask-like visage her hair was gathered up from the nape of the neck into an enormous, weighty decoration of jewels, shaped like flowers and insects, which fanned out on either side and hung down with tassels of pearls. She wore the Manchu costume of tunic and trousers in vivid silk and her shoes had a central high wedge hung with pearls and encrusted with jewels.

But she was only one of 3,000 concubines and 3,000 eunuchs whose lives were dedicated to the dissolute 20-year-old Emperor, Hsien-Feng. She was of the fifth and lowest rank and it was quite likely that she would never even meet him, but would spend her days as an exalted servant. Given the name Imperial Concubine Yi she set out to make what she could of her position. The palace had a fine library and as, unlike most girls, she had learned to read and write, she took every advantage of the books and scholarly tutors now available to her. She also befriended and flattered the 15-year-old concubine of higher ancestry who had been chosen to be Hsien-Feng's wife.

After three years her cunning was rewarded. The Empress proved barren and one night she was sent for to share the Emperor's bed. Nine months later, in April 1856, she gave birth to a son, his Imperial Majesty's only male child.

Her status was immediately enhanced. The powerful eunuchs, who infiltrated and dominated court life with their intrigue and malicious gossip, sensed a new star rising and gathered round her. Tzu-hsi never under-estimated their influence and enjoyed their silken subservience. Hsien-Feng was amazed at his new concubine's grasp of affairs and her dynamic energy and in the end found it easier to let her take part in politics and run things for him. Effeminate, weak and ill he seemed unable to cope with the terrible wars launched by the Taiping rebels in the north. When these troubles were added to by an invasion of North China by joint forces of England and France, it was the last straw.

To escape the advancing 'foreign devils' the royal court fled from Peking to Jehol, away in the mountains. Signs of a shift in power came with a special decree from the royal palace ordering the decapitation of all prisoners as a warning to the 'bandits' who had dared to invade the Forbidden City. The voice that gave that order was not the Emperor's but that of the Concubine Yi.

Blood flowed in Peking but Hsien-Feng's brother, the statesmanlike Prince Kung, was wise enough to realize that the killing of Europeans could not go on. China's only hope lay in submission. He ignored further imperial decrees and made a peace treaty with the French and English.

The Emperor was to return to his capital in the spring of 1861 but before the winter storms had ceased, he was dead. His Empress and Tzu-hsi became regents. At the first sign of good weather they set out on the long, stony road from Jehol to Peking, taking the child Emperor with them. They had been warned of a plot by conspiritors who wanted to seize power and who planned to kill the two regents and leave their bodies for the vultures. The royal route over the wild mountain passes was changed at the last minute.

All eyes were on Tzu-hsi as she made a triumphal entry into Peking with her son, borne shoulder high on a yellow throne through streets hung with yellow banners and strewn with yellow sand.

This was the point at which she had to decide who were her friends and who were her enemies. The Empress Niuhuru had no interest in political power, so could be discounted. But Tzu-hsi gave orders immediately that Su Shun, the wealthy man behind the assassination plot, was to be decapitated and his supporters ordered to commit suicide. She grabbed his estates and laid the foundations of an immense fortune.

Civil war at its most terrible raged through five provinces and 20 million people died in the first years of her reign, as the Taiping rebellion continued to run its terrible course in the mountains of the north. During these years she relied heavily on the wisdom of Prince Kung. He saw her every day, taught her state craft and did his best to curb her war-like tendencies.

At first their meetings were conducted with the strictest formality and etiquette. As time went by, however, Prince Kung became a little too familiar for Tzu-hsi's liking. She had had enough of the pupil-teacher relationship and decided to get rid of him.

Her moment came in the fourth year of her regency. One day Prince Kung absentmindedly started to rise from his knees during a long and tedious audience. (A judicial rule of etiquette forbade anyone to stand in the sovereign's presence to safeguard against attack). Tzu-hsi shrieked for help, worked herself into a terrible rage and claimed that he had moved towards the throne to attack her. He was seized by eunuchs, dragged from her presence and stripped of all honours and duties.

Later, probably because she could not do without him, she extended her forgiveness and he was re-admitted to the Grand Council. But she had made her point. She had brought down the most powerful man in the country, and subjugated him to her will.

Her private life became more and more extravagant and she encouraged her officials to increase taxes on an already impoverished Chinese people in order to keep the Dragon Court in feudal magnificence. Still not satisfied she began selling all positions of authority for large donations to her coffers.

Meanwhile, the young Emperor, Tung Cheh, was being brought up in a hot-house environment dominated by painted concubines and eunuchs. It was as though Tzu-hsi was plotting his downfall from the very beginning, looking ahead to the day when he assumed power and she would no longer be needed. She indulged the eunuchs and took no notice of the terrible influence they had on him from the earliest age. By fifteen it was obvious that he had all his father's ambi-sexual tastes and was steeped in debauchery. The eunuchs planned orgies and she encouraged them to introduce him to the whores in the back streets of Peking.

By 1872, when he was 16, he was considered old enough to marry and daughters of Manchu officials were ordered to appear at the Palace. He chose as his bride a beautiful 18-year-old girl called Alute who proved to have brains as well as looks. Tzu-hsi became fiercely jealous of her and extremely angry when she realized that Alute was encouraging the wretched Tung Cheh to think for himself and resist the influence of the eunuchs. But it was too late.

When the time came for the young Emperor to assume the throne officially and for Tzu-hsi to retire and do her embroidery, her chagrin was felt in every corner of the Forbidden City. She gave orders that the old Imperial Summer Palace, destroyed by the British and French, should be rebuilt for her in all its glory. Vast sums were raised for the purpose but many, Prince Kung among them, complained of such extravagance while China was still suffering from the terrible results of the Taiping rebellion. The rebuilding was abandoned and Tzu-hsi shut herself away in fury.

She did not have long to wait. The Emperor's exploits with the whores and transvestites of Peking were beginning to take their toll. He was found to be suffering from venereal disease then his weakened frame succumbed to smallpox. Little was done to help him. In the flowery language of the court, he 'Ascended the Dragon' on 13 January 1875. He was only 19.

His loving Empress, Alute, had never left his bedside. Tzu-hsi hearing her complain to him of her overbearing ways flew into one of her terrible rages and ordered the eunuchs to take her away and beat her. Alute was pregnant and there was no doubt among court officials that Tzu-hsi had made up her mind to get rid of the girl before the birth of her child.

On the day of her son's death, sitting on the Dragon throne with the compliant Niuhuru by her side, she called a Grand Council. Tung had left no heir. An Emperor had to be chosen. Sweeping aside all tradition she insisted it should be her nephew, the son of her only sister. She was flagrantly manipulating the ancient dynastic law and only ten men dared to defy her. She made a note of their names. She could not stand opposition and had unscrupulous methods of getting rid of those who stood in her path.

She immediately adopted her nephew, Kuang-hsu. The thin, delicate three-year-old was fetched in the middle of the night, hastily dressed in imperial robes and taken to pay homage at the bier of his dead cousin. On 25 February 1875 he became Emperor. Tzu-hsi knew she could remain in power as regent for another decade at least. The neglected, humiliated Empress Alute, denied the succession for her expected child and made ill by her mother-in-law's treatment, killed herself with an overdose of opium. It was even said in some quarters that Tzu-hsi had ordered her to commit suicide because her presence was repugnant to her.

With the arrival of Kuang-hsu unexpected rivalry grew up between the two regents. The child was obviously terrified of Tzu-hsi and much preferred the gentle Niuhuru. Stories vary as to the actual nature of the dispute which finally brought about the latter's death, but it is known that one afternoon Tzu-hsi sent her some rice cakes, and by the evening she was dead.

After that the Dragon Empress ruled alone as regent for six years, her constant companion being the chief eunuch, Li Lien Ying, a corrupt, avaricious, cruel man who was, nevertheless, utterly devoted to her. She totally dominated the young emperor, a languid, listless youth with 'a voice like a mosquito'. He was said to have been frightened of her and one can understand why. A court official, describing her rage said; 'Her eyes poured out straight rays, her cheekbones were sharp and the veins on her forehead projected. She showed her teeth. . . .'

In 1887 Kuang-hsu attained his majority and the regent, now 55, went into retirement. She chose a luxurious retreat just outside Peking, where she could keep a close watch on him. What she saw amazed her. The Emperor was not the puppet she had supposed. He had, in fact, a thirst for Western knowledge and ideas and visions of ending the repressive regime he had inherited and creating something nearer to European democracies. Tzu-hsi had married him to her niece, a bad tempered, plain girl who created trouble from the start. He much preferred his two senior concubines, Pearl and Lustrous, who were educated women and had sympathy with his ideas.

Though he always treated her with great respect, Tzu-hsi came to hate him for his outward looking politics. There was only one sort of China for her and that was the China of her ancestors. She set her chief eunuch to spy on him and blamed him for China's humiliating war with Japan whereas the blame in fact lay at her doorstep for she had ruined the navy by taking funds.

Great bitterness developed between Tzu-hsi and her nephew. At last he decided the only solution was to kill her favourite, Jung Lu, and imprison her. But he was betrayed by officials who feared what changes the coup might bring and instead found himself a prisoner.

The Dragon Empress

The enraged Dowager Empress as she was now called, dared not kill him but had all his attendants put to death or banished and replaced them with her own. Pearl, Kuang-hsu's concubine, knelt before her imploring her to spare the Emperor further humiliation. She even dared to suggest that as Kuang-hsu was the lawful sovreign anyway she had no right to set aside the mandate of heaven. Tzu-hsi dismissed her and had her imprisoned.

As for the pitiful young Emperor with his dreams of a better world, his reign was virtually ended. She kept him in solitary confinement and re-instated herself as regent. But the rest of the world was becoming interested in China, which had been a closed book for centuries, and there was great sympathy for Kuang-hsu. The British Minister went so far as to say that foreign countries would view with displeasure and alarm his sudden demise. She was incensed by this sympathy for him and her old hatred of 'foreign devils' began to fester.

The Boxer movement started among gangs of reactionary youths in the Kuan district of Shantung. They were violently anti-foreign and derived their name from the gymnastic exercises and shadow boxing they performed to work themselves into a frenzy. Their blood chilling rites and ceremonies were accompanied by cries of 'Exterminate the barbarians.' But as they were fiercely loyal to the Ch'ing Dynasty and fanatically nationalistic, Tzu-hsi chose to regard them as a 'people's army' and gave them support.

Soon the killing and the burning began. No missionary or Chinese convert was safe. Some of her ministers dared to warn all Europeans to get out while they could; they were beheaded. When a dispatch came from the foreign ministers demanding her immediate abdication and the restoration of the Kuang Emperor she roared 'How dare they question my authority – let us exterminate them.'

Appalled by what was going on, foreign governments made plans to invade China and rescue those who were holding out, mostly in the only important European building left standing – the British Legation. An international force landed and captured Tientsin, then started moving up the railway line to Peking. The Dowager Empress watched with dismay as turmoil grew in the city and people began fleeing to the hills. As foreign troops drew nearer she made no attempt to control what was happening but made plans to leave with the Emperor.

All the concubines were ordered to appear before her, the Emperor's favourite, Pearl, among them. The unfortunate girl who had still not learned her lesson, suggested that the Emperor's place was in Peking. Tzu-hsi was in no mood for argument. 'Throw this wretched minion down the well' she ordered. Pushing aside Kuang-hsu who fell on his knees pleading with her to spare the concubine's life, she ordered 'Let her die at once.' There was certainly no time to waste. The enemy was at the gates. Dressed as peasants and riding on an old cart, Tzu-hsi and her nephew fled Peking.

For the first time in her life the Dowager Empress began to experience what it was like to live as an ordinary Chinese. During the first days in exile she had to sleep like the poorest traveller in wretched, flea-ridden inns and eat the coarse common porridge made from millet. She saw the suffering of peasant families and professed pity for them, handing out gifts of money, and saying she had not appreciated their plight in the seclusion of her palace.

But she did not have to share their life for long. Even in exile she was soon surrounded by luxury. With great relief she heard on 1 June 1901 that peace terms had been agreed and she could fix a date for the court's return. Fully convinced that she would be exempt from blame, she left for Peking in a blaze of pageantry with silk banners, painted lanterns and flowers. Before she entered the city she made offerings to the river god.

She gradually managed to convince herself that she had nothing to do with the atrocities and greeted every foreigner she met with the utmost charm and civility. She demanded that history be rewritten and all decrees favouring the Boxers wiped from the records. At last she realized the full power of the western world and in the last few years of her life issued edicts that brought about major reforms that even Kuang-hsu would have approved.

The Emperor had been badly treated ever since their return from exile. He was given insolent eunuchs to serve him, provided with stale and unpalatable food and when the rest of the palace was converted to electricity, his apartments were left out.

But the end was very near for both of them, an extraordinary end that could have been a twist of fate but was more likely due to human venom.

In the summer of 1907 the Dowager Empress suffered a slight stroke and the following year became weak and ill with dysentry. Her usually robust health seemed to be failing. As she took to her bed, the Emperor became desperately ill and took to his. He was suffering from a disease of the kidneys and his health was ruined, but the doctor who was fetched to see him found him writhing in agony and suffering from symptoms he had never seen before. Kuang-hsu lay back on his satin cushions and died early in the morning on 14 November 1908. Before he died he scribbled a curse on the woman who had put him on the throne.

Twenty-four hours later Tzu-hsi asked for the traditional robe of longevity, turned her face to the south, and died. Those present said when told of the Emperor's death she had seemed relieved. Had she, in a last act of hatred had him poisoned? No one could be quite sure.

She was buried with great splendour. Twenty years after her funeral bandits broke into her tomb and stole the treasure that had been buried with her. Her body was carelessly flung to one side.

Chapter Five

Female Fanatics

When a woman becomes obsessed, nothing is allowed to stand in her way. The object of her passion may be a man or a cause but the outcome of her obsession is seldom a happy one....

Ulrike Meinhof

Early in the evening of 16 June 1972 a tense German policeman, acting on a tip-off, knocked at the door of a flat in the suburban village of Langenhagen, near Hanover airport.

The door was opened by a sullen looking woman with straggling hair, who immediately realized her mistake. Suddenly police were swarming everywhere. She struggled hysterically, fought and shouted obscenities. But it was all over for Ulrike Meinhof.

After the biggest and most sustained search in German police history, the middle class anarchist who had come to be regarded as the most dangerous woman in Europe, was in their grasp. As she was led away they opened one of her suitcases, packed for a flight from Hanover airport. They were not really surprised to find it contained three 9 mm pistols, two hand grenades, one submachine gun and a ten pound bomb.

With university drop-out, Andreas Baader, as her partner, Ulrike had been waging war on the established order for nearly three years. The terrorist group they formed committed so many crimes, ranging from murder to forgery, that it needed 354 pages to list them when they came to trial. Baader and two other gang leaders were already in prison. But until that June evening when Ulrike Meinhof was captured, the authorities could not rest for she was undoubtedly the intellect, the driving force behind everything.

The story of how she changed from an idealistic student into a fanatical anarchist ready to tear down everybody and everything is full of violence and hatred. Yet in the middle of it she remains a sad figure.

Ulrike Meinhof was born into an intellectual, upper middle class family at Oldenburg, Lower Saxony, on 7 October 1934. Both her parents were art historians but her father died when she was only five, her mother when she was 14. During her formative years she was fostered by her mother's friend, Professor Renate Riemeck, an intellectual woman of strong radical views. It was said that Ulrike learned from her many of her socialist ideas and the importance of never accepting the edicts of authority without first questioning them.

The attractive, red haired girl soon showed signs of academic brilliance. In 1957, when she was 23, she went to Munster University to study sociology and philosophy. She campaigned against the atom bomb, the Americans in Vietnam and most of the burning issues that radical minded students were interested in.

One day she was introduced to a thin faced, handsome man called Klaus Roehl. He ran a lively, left wing magazine called *Konkret* and when he asked her to join its staff she agreed.

Before long Ulrike had acquired a reputation as a first class radical journalist, writing columns of such brilliance that she began to be talked about in circles outside the university. She probed into the economy of Germany, dealt with social questions many people felt were being brushed under the carpet and wrote about the misery that existed among those who had no part in Germany's so called Economic Miracle.

Klaus Roehl made her his editor and his wife.

The magazine was successful enough in its own way, but not a best seller. When Roehl hit on the idea of adding sex to the political content, it took off. They made a lot of money, lived in a fashionable house and drove round in a large white Mercedes.

Ulrike, now the mother of twin daughters, found herself the darling of radical chic society and became a familiar face on television. But the success and the gloss were superficial and inwardly Ulrike was burning with resentment. Her husband, she had discovered, was a womaniser. His affairs became too much for her and after seven years together, they were divorced.

She gave up her job with her marriage, moved to Berlin and put her daughters, Regine and Bettina, into an old fashioned, strict discipline boarding school. This left her free to mix with a group of well-off young people with extreme radical views, who believed the only way to change society was through violence. The idea took root. She was soon publicly defending arson, violent protest and the crimes of urban guerillas. But before she acted politically she had to get rid of some personal bitterness. She started a campaign against her husband and his magazine which culminated in a night of fury in which she and her friends vandalised the home in which she had once taken such a pride.

Through the grapevine she heard a lot about a young agitator and arsonist called Andreas Baader who was serving a prison sentence for his part in burning down a Frankfurt department store. One day she met Baader's 'revolutionary bride', a tall, blonde girl called Gudrun Ensslin, a pastor's daughter, who had studied philosophy. Gudrun told her his friends were determined to get him out and they wanted her to help. On certain days he was allowed to work outside the prison in a Berlin library, and it was decided to 'spring him' from there. On 14 May 1970 Ulrike led the raid with a gang of armed terrorists, leaving the librarian severely wounded and several prison guards with bullet holes. The violence had started.

After Andreas and Ulrike had had time to sum each other up, they agreed to form the Baader-Meinhof gang with a hard core of about 24 fellow anarchists. Apart from themselves the leading members would be Baader's girl friend, Gudrun, and Jan Carl Raspe, who became Ulrike's lover.

Andreas Baader was officially the leader of the group. He was a dark, brooding, handsome man, attractive to women, who based his image on the young Marlon Brando. He was also indolent, spoiled and aggressive. Ulrike Meinhof supplied the drive and the brains in their partnership.

The four of them managed to flee the country after the raid and turned up in the Middle East to train with the Palestine National Liberation Front. But the Germans and Arabs did not get on too well, each accusing the other of being cold and arrogant. The two women were considered domineering and a damned nuisance and before long the PLO decided that their trainees were rebels without a true cause and asked them to leave.

Ulrike remained passionately pro-Palestinian. On her return to Germany she made the shocking decision to send her two small daughters to a refugee camp in Jordan to be trained along with Palestinian children to become *kamikaze* fighters against Israel. Fortunately for them, her plans went wrong. Karl Roehl had been scouring Germany for his children and had even engaged private detectives. He was tipped off just in time and they were snatched from a hideout in Palermo. They hated him at first because their mother's indoctrination had been very thorough. But for all his faults he was a good and devoted father and won back their affection.

The gang grew to be about 150 strong all told. Most of its members were from quite prosperous backgrounds, the only two working class recruits being garage hands, useful for dealing with stolen cars.

They were armed to the teeth with small fire arms, submachine guns, hand grenades and bombs and set out on a series of bank raids and robberies to raise funds to buy more. There was one particularly terrible assault on a branch of the Bavarian Mortgage and Exchange Bank in the small provincial town of Kaiserslautern, 35 miles west of Heidelberg, in which a police officer was murdered with callous deliberation.

Taking part in the raid was a new recruit, a long haired blonde called Ingeborg Barz. The girl was so horrified by the bloodshed that she made up her mind to go home. She telephoned her parents in Berlin. It was the last they ever heard of her. According to Gerhart Muller, who turned state witness, she was summoned to a meeting with Ulrike Meinhof then driven to a remote spot near some gravel pits where she was executed.

Violence piled upon violence while the ordinary man in the street watched with horror. During two years of urban terror five people were shot or blown to bits, there were 54 attempted murders, countless vicious assaults and a series of bombings directed against the American Army in Germany. Ulrike had developed a complete disregard for human life and categorized some

FEMALE FANATICS

Ulrike Meinhof

people, including policemen, as 'pigs'. Her aspirations were supposed to be humane; to do something about the injustices she saw in human society. In fact she seemed to be using terrorism to work out of her system a load of hatred and bitterness.

The police put all their manpower into an attempt to crack the terrorist hold on West Germany and their chance came one day early in 1972 in a quiet Frankfurt Street. They had received an anonymous tip that a garage there was stuffed with ammunition. They drove up in two lorries, loaded with sandbags and began to build a wall – but because they were dressed in overalls they looked more like corporation gardeners delivering bags of peat. After a time a smart lilac coloured Porsche drew up. Three young men in leather jackets climbed out. Two of them went into the garage, the third, waiting outside on the pavement was grabbed by the police. They found they had got Carl Raspe the arch terrorist who was also Ulrike's lover. After a long, tense seige, first a gang member called Holger Meins was brought out. Then, after a brief exchange of fire the police dragged out a dark young man writhing with pain from a bullet in the thigh. It was Andreas Baader.

Not long after Gudrun Ensslin was captured in a Hamburg dress shop when a shop assistant discovered a gun in her jacket and phoned the police. Ulrike began to feel very much alone. As the months went by she found that even her friends from the trendy left felt she was too dangerous to be associated with.

Then came the night in June when she decided to head for Hanover airport. She knew a left wing teacher who had a flat nearby and turned up on his doorstep with several suitcases. He was in a terrible dilemma. He now held a respected position as Federal President of the Teachers' Union. The last thing he wanted was Ulrike Meinhof as house guest. He went to seek the advice of some friends and they urged him to phone the police at once. He made the phone call and stayed clear of the flat....

The rest of Ulrike's life was to be spent in prison or in the courtroom where she yelled and shouted abuse at her judges. The trial of the Baader-Meinhof gang was considered so potentially explosive that a fortified courtroom and special cells were built at the top security prison at Stammheim in Stuttgart. There was great fear that reprisals and counter measures would be launched by terrorists still outside.

Though members of the gang were kept apart she became aware as the trial went on of the enmity of the others, especially in the case of Gudrun Ensslin. Solitary, apart from her typewriter and her books, she began to brood. Eventually the pressure must have become too great. On the morning of 9 May 1976 she was found hanging in her cell.

Her followers refused to believe that she had committed suicide and for a time insisted she had been murdered by the authorities. Four thousand people marched in the cortège at her funeral in Berlin, many of them masked to avoid identification. The police felt they were watching over a time bomb and later they had to deal with revenge terrorist attacks.

But of Ulrike Meinhof a priest who knew her said afterwards 'I think she finally decided she had come to the end of the wrong road....'

Mary Tudor

Henry VIII's elder daughter has been condemned to be known for all time as 'Bloody Mary'. Her face with its tight, narrow lips and short sighted eyes, peers out at us from Tudor portraits with frightening intensity. Even so, it is hard to imagine how in the short years of her reign this pious woman left England reeling as she sought to gain her religious ends by acts of appaling cruelty and fanaticism.

By the time she came to the throne in 1553, Mary Tudor was an embittered woman of 37. She suffered from a disorder of the womb, complained of violent headaches and had a deep rooted aversion to sex. She had survived some traumatic experiences but instead of making her aware of the sufferings of others she had become hardened. It soon became clear that she would let nothing stand in the way of her one great passion – the restoration of the Roman Catholic Church and the supremacy of the Pope in England.

Gathering her forces round her she began her reign of terror against the Protestants with an order that the neglected statutes against heretics were to be brought back into full use. She gave her commissioners power to investigate all rumours of heresy and to arrest offenders on the spot. Protestant homes were broken into, premises searched for heretical books and torture used on men and women alike.

But the real horror began one February morning in 1555 when the first Protestant martyr was tied to the stake at Smithfield and perished in full view of his wife and children. Before her own death four years later, Mary was to be responsible for committing 283 martyrs to the terrible death by fire. At the worst period there was an average of one burning every five days. She seemed to be a woman without mercy.

So obsessed was she with rooting out heretics that she allowed the country's economy to get into an appalling state. Prices were so high that people were driven through hunger to grind acorns for bread meal and to make do with water instead of the universal drink – ale. Mary thought it far more important to concern herself with the spiritual needs of her subjects rather than their general welfare. As the flames rose higher and higher, so did people's anger. She had to abandon any plan for showing herself on royal 'progresses' as other Tudor monarchs had done. She became so hated that her safety could not be guaranteed.

Yet when Mary Tudor first ascended the throne the bells of London rang out joyously and people stood for hours in the streets to cheer as she passed on her way to Westminster. She was a heroine in many eyes for the way she had borne so many injustices and for the way in which she had stood firm against her royal father's tyranny.

Born at Greenwich on 18 February, 1516, the daughter of Henry VIII and his first wife, Catherine of Aragon, Mary was out of favour from the start. She should have been a boy. Though Henry showed his disappointment he seems to have been fond of her as a child and saw to it that she had a good, classical education. Her misery began with the appearance at court of the beautiful, bewitching Anne Boleyn. Henry, passionately in love with her was determined somehow to obtain a divorce and make her his wife. How many people he hurt and destroyed in the process was of no importance.

Cranmer was appointed Archbishop of Canterbury and the King ordered him to sit as a judge and try his divorce case. Catherine refused to recognize the court or to appear before, it, but Cranmer still gave judgement that her marriage to Henry had been unlawful. This meant that Mary was considered a bastard and had no right to the throne. She never forgave Cranmer and in spite of the fact that his intervention probably saved her from the Tower, she later had her revenge and sent him to the stake.

When Henry married Anne Boleyn in January 1533 and she gave birth to the future Queen Elizabeth the following autumn, Mary was told she must no longer call herself Princess and she was to give precedence to Anne Boleyn's daughter at all times. She was forcibly parted from the mother she loved and had every pressure put on her to make her renounce her Catholic faith.

Both Queen Catherine, isolated with her Spanish ladies-in-waiting at a cold and cheerless manor at Kimbolton in Northamptonshire, and Mary, placed in charge of Anne Boleyn's sister at Hatfield in Hertfordshire, went in fear of their lives. Each morning when they woke they dreaded being forced to take the Oath of Succession declaring that Anne's children were heirs to the throne or the Oath of Supremacy declaring Henry supreme head of the Church in England. There was a great deal of sympathy for them throughout the country especially when it became known that Queen Catherine had died on 7 January 1536, still declaring her love for the King but without Mary being allowed to visit her, write to her or receive any momento.

Mary still stubbornly refused to bend to her father's will. Throughout this period her only ally was her mother's nephew, the powerful Emperor Charles V of Spain. His ambassador to England, Eustace Chapuys frequently tried to intervene on her behalf when he thought her in danger and at the same time warned her that unless she tempered her fierce Tudor pride with a little humility, she might lose her head. Many believed that it was only the fact that the powerful Emperor of Spain knew of her danger and had sympathy for her that kept her head on her shoulders. Mary did at one time consider escape to Spain but her heart was not in it. What she really wanted was for Charles V to invade England.

Things began to improve for her when Anne Boleyn was sent to the block for adultery and Henry married the gentle Jane Seymour, daughter of a Wiltshire knight. The new Queen felt pity for Mary and advised her for her own sake to show humility and beg Henry's forgiveness. Eventually after being urged by Chapuys, who told her she was 'the most obstinate and obdurate woman, all things considered that ever was', she agreed to sign the papers acknowledging her parents divorce. Six months later she returned to Greenwich.

On the day before Anne Boleyn was beheaded Cranmer obligingly annulled her marriage to Henry in a farcical trial. This made both Mary and Elizabeth bastards. So when, on 12 October 1537, Jane Seymour gave birth to a son who would become King Edward VI, Mary, in good temper, recognized that her new brother took precedence over her and she did in fact become very fond of him.

For the next decade she lived at court when she was in her father's favour and in confinement in some isolated castle whenever there was an upsurge of Catholic feeling in the country. There was an attempt to marry her to the Duke of Orleans but it came to nothing.

One bitterly cold night at the end of January 1547, the tyrant Henry died and the throne passed to his frail but staunchly Protestant son.

It was clear from the beginning that Edward would not live for very long. He had a mind of his own and an affectionate nature, but power lay in the hands of his uncle, Edward Seymour, Jane Seymour's brother, who became Lord Protector and with Cranmer set out to firmly establish England as a Protestant country. This made it extremely difficult for Mary to remain at court in spite of her fond relationship with her brother, so she retired again to the country and was allowed to say mass in private.

By the summer of 1553 the whole country knew that Edward was dying. He had survived serious attacks of measles and smallpox but his constitution

Mary Tudor

was weakened and he succumbed to tuberculosis. Mary diligently prepared herself to take up her duties for by Act of Parliament and under Henry's will, she was next in line to the throne. First, however she had to contend with one of the most shameful power struggles in English history.

It was led by the corrupt and unscrupulous Duke of Northumberland, who was determined to keep Mary from the throne in order to preserve his own power and the power of the Protestant nobles. His pawn was the poor little innocent Lady Jane Grey. She was cousin to the young King and third in succession after Mary and Elizabeth. Northumberland married her to his son, Lord Guildford Dudley, then persuaded Edward to make a will bequeathing her the crown and excluding both Mary and Elizabeth on the grounds that they were illegitimate. The dying King, anxious to support Northumberland and his Protestant cause, signed away his sister's birthright.

When Lady Jane Grey was told that she was to be Queen of England she fainted from shock. She protested she had no desire for the crown. But even her own father, the cowardly Duke of Suffolk who changed sides as often as he changed coats, pushed her on to her tragic destiny. She was only to reign for nine days.

Meanwhile Mary's supporters were rallying to her at Framlingham Castle in Suffolk. Added to them were thousands who hated Northumberland. Soon it became obvious that a movement to put Mary on the throne was gathering momentum and when they saw which way the tide was flowing all the leading nobles and officials, including those who had fervently supported Lady Jane Grey, scurried to Framlingham to acknowledge Mary as their rightful queen and to beg for her pardon.

On 19 July 1553 she was proclaimed in London. She made a slow and dignified progress towards the capital, receiving Elizabeth on the way, then entering the city in triumph. People cheered, sang and danced in the streets, but little did they know that the fountains which were filled with wine would soon run with blood. On 1 October Mary was crowned at Westminster by the Catholic Bishop Stephen Gardiner, Cranmer having been already sent to the Tower.

Mary set about disposing of those who had acted against her. It soon became clear that she was prepared to be ruthless and though her accession had seemed popular with the masses in spite of the religious problem, those close to her began to urge her to marry to reinforce her position. Her old friend and protector Charles v put forward his own son, Prince Philip of Spain as a suitable husband. Mary's dislike of sex made her very reluctant to take this step, especially as Philip was only 26, 11 years younger than herself, and reported to be virile. Charles sent Renard, his ambassador and one of the most skilful and cunning diplomats in Europe to persuade her. When finally she agreed it was only to find her choice so unpopular from a political point of view that riots broke out all over the country. The most serious of these revolts was led by a 23-year-old Catholic, Sir Thomas Wyatt supported by an army of 15,000. They actually reached the city before being crushed.

Shaken and angry, Mary's attitude hardened towards those she considered her enemies. Although she had accepted Lady Jane Grey as a pawn of ambitious men she now saw her as a dangerous focal point for rebellion. Dressed in black from head to foot, the pathetic 16-year-old girl was executed as a traitor.

Unrest in England had only made Mary more determined to proceed with her plans. Philip landed at Southampton in July 1554 'in a wild wind and down-pouring rain'. They were married at Winchester Cathedral having only set eyes on each other once before. Philip, a dazzling, handsome figure in white was kept waiting for half an hour before Mary arrived, resplendent in cloth of gold. She fell deeply in love with him but he found her so unattractive that one of his friends remarked sympathetically 'It would take God himself to drink this cup'. Philip was gallant and attentive to her in public but privately admitted the marriage was a failure and that she lacked 'all sensibility of the flesh'. Soon rumours of his amorous intrigues were all over London. During their marriage she twice declared herself pregnant and had a *Te Deum* of thanks sung in churches all over London. But it proved to be only a disease of the womb that made her swell like a pregnant woman. At this point of her life she was truly to be pitied.

But the stage was being set for the last dreadful years of her life. Ambassador Renard had been instructed by Charles v to urge Mary to be ruthless in punishing traitors and ridding herself of political enemies but he also begged her to try to restrain her religious fervour and to proceed cautiously in restoring the Catholic religion and persecuting Protestants. She turned a deaf ear to his wishes.

The victimisation of Protestants began only a few months after her wedding when the statutes against heretics came into force. The Bishop of London, Edmund Bonner, who with Bishop Gardiner was the Queen's chief prosecutor, led a procession through the streets of London to celebrate the restoration of Rome's power. A tribunal was set up at Southwark to examine suspected heretics.

The first martyr of her reign, the married priest, John Rogers, burned at Smithfield in February 1555 was soon followed by others. That same week Lawrence Saunders, Rector of All Hallows, Coventry, Dr Rowland Taylor of Hadleigh and Bishop Hooper of Gloucester also went to the stake. No one could understand why Mary allowed Hooper to be burned. He had always been loyal to her in spite of their religious differences. In the course of the year most of the Protestant bishops and leading theologians who had not escaped abroad were sent to the fire. By the end of it, the toll had reached 90. They included men like Hugh Latimer, Bishop of Worcester, who with Cranmer had taken part in establishing the Protestant church and Ridley, Bishop of London, who had supported Lady Jane Grey. The two of them were taken to Oxford, chained back to back and tied to the stake. As the flames rose Latimer cried out in immortal words 'Play the man, Master Ridley. We shall this day light such a candle in England as by the Grace of God shall never be put out!' Latimer died quickly but poor Ridley suffered a terrible death as the fire on his side was slow burning. After Latimer and Ridley came Archbishop Cranmer who signed six recantations on the promise of a pardon but in the end found the courage to stand by what he truly believed. He was said to have met his end with fortitude.

Most of the Protestant martyrs however were simple folk, more than half of them coming from London, Kent and Essex. There was a great outcry as the burnings went on for though this method of dealing with heresy had been accepted in earlier reigns it had never been on this scale. Mary could have stopped the terrible deaths at any time but it seemed as though mercy and pity had died in her. Her supporters claimed that she was encouraged by her Spanish husband but in fact he argued moderation because he knew these Inquisition-like executions would not be accepted by the English temperament.

Philip, though considerate and courteous, had become increasingly disenchanted with his wife and secretly appalled at what was happening in England. Mary looked old for her age. Though not yet 40 her complexion was heavily wrinkled, her mouth thin and tight. She was very short sighted and would sometimes stare at people for a long time in a way that frightened them. Her court had become increasingly sombre as though in perpetual mourning and though her own clothes were rich and her jewels rare she took no pleasure in them. She never slept for more than three or four hours a night, went to mass nine times a day and worked hard on her state papers. But she was still in love with her husband and when Philip announced he had to leave England for a time to deal with his territories abroad, Mary wept bitterly.

With Philip gone, her barren condition known to everyone, Mary turned with wrath on her heretics. She introduced a new and terrible element into the persecutions. Heretics would no longer be given an opportunity to recant before they died. Many people, though not prepared to be martyrs themselves, began to regard those who went to the stake as saints. They would touch them as they went to their deaths and ask for a blessing. This made Mary so angry she declared that anyone showing compassion for a heretic at the stake was to be arrested. A man in Norwich who protested against the agony he saw was flogged through the streets.

To Mary's great joy Philip returned to England in March 1557, but it was not for love of her. His reason was political. During the three months of his stay he persuaded her, against the advice of her ministers, to join him in declaring war on France. Mary never forgave herself for allowing herself to be drawn into this war. Through it she lost Calais, which had been part of England for more than 200 years.

In the spring of 1558 Mary became seriously ill. She seems to have suffered from dropsy and, some say, a malignant growth of the womb. Certainly she was in a desperate way and also suffering from melancholia. Most of the time she spent weeping for Philip, for Calais and for her cause. It was becoming increasingly obvious that her policy of suppressing heresy had not been successful. Secret prayer meetings were being held everywhere, forbidden books circulated and more and more vocal demonstrations held in support of the martyrs. When seven people were burned at Smithfield in the summer of that year a large crowd cheered and sang hymns.

Mary raved about all that was reported to her but as the year turned to winter and its darkest days, she began to sink rapidly. On 10 November she signed the order for five heretics to be burned at Canterbury. They were to be the last victims of her reign. Three days later, though she knew herself to be near to death she found the strength to sign the death warrant of two more London Protestants. They were the luckiest men in England. There was no time to carry out the order. Mary died at four o'clock in the morning on 17 November. At daybreak the two men were set free and sent home to their wives.

Elizabeth began her glorious reign by giving Mary a Catholic funeral of great splendour, but the Catholic cause in England did not recover from her fanatical cruelty for centuries to come.

Elizabeth Bathory

The Countess Elizabeth Bathory who lived in the Carpathian mountains in the 16th century was one of the original vampires who inspired Bram Stoker's legend of Dracula.

She was Hungarian by birth. Records give her entry into the world as

Countess Elizabeth Bathory

1561. As a girl she was beautiful with long fair hair and an exquisite complexion. She was married off to an aristocratic soldier when she was fifteen and became mistress of the Castle of Csejthe in the Carpathians.

Life in the dark, gloomy Csejthe Castle, while her husband was away on his various military campaigns, became very boring indeed. She was determined to liven things up.

First she gathered round her a sinister band of witches, sorcerers and alchemists who taught her the black arts. Then, armed with her special flesh-tearing silver pincers, a manual of tortures her husband had used when fighting the Turks and a taste for flagellation learned from her aunt, she set out to indulge herself and while away the lonely hours.

When her husband died in 1604 she had reached the difficult age of 43. She longed for a new lover to replace him but her reflection in the mirror showed her that time and indulgence had not improved her looks. One day she slapped the face of a servant girl and drew blood with her nails. She was convinced that that part of her body where the girl's blood had dripped was much fresher and younger than before. It only needed the alchemists to add their opinion and she was convinced that drinking and bathing in the blood of young virgins would preserve her beauty for ever.

So, at the dead of night, the Countess and her cronies would tear about the countryside hunting for girls. They would be taken back to the castle, hung in chains and their blood used for the countess' bath, the finest saved for her to drink.

The terrible woman carried on like this for five years until she began to realize the blood of peasant girls had not been terribly effective. In 1609 she turned to the daughters of her own class. Offering to take in 25 girls at a time to teach them social graces, she soon had a flourishing academy.

Helped as usual by her peasant procuress, Dorotta Szentes, know as Dorka, she treated the 'pupils' with the same inhuman cruelty as she had treated the others. But this time she became too careless. The bodies of four girls were thrown over the castle walls. Before she realized her mistake villagers collected them and took them away to be identified. Her secret was out.

News of her reign of terror finally reached the ears of the Hungarian Emperor, Matthias II. He ordered that the Countess be brought to trial. But as an aristocrat she could not be arrested, so Parliament passed a new Act so that she would not be able to slip throught their hands. At her hearing in 1610 it was said she had murdered 600 girls.

Dorka and her witches were burnt at the stake. The Countess escaped execution because of her noble birth. But she was condemned to a living death – walled up in a tiny room of her castle and kept alive by scraps of food pushed through the bars. She died four years later without a word of remorse.

Lady Caroline Lamb

After Lady Caroline Lamb met Lord Byron for the first time she summed him up in her diary as 'Mad, bad and dangerous to know'. Looking into the poet's handsome face she felt faint and had to turn away.

Nine months later it was he who was tempted to say the same thing about her for she had driven him frantic with her obsession for him – 'Let me be quiet. Leave me alone,' he wailed in most uncharacteristic tones for such an infamous womaniser.

A dainty, delicate sprite with fair curls clinging to her head she was in many ways an altogether delightful creature when she wasn't tearing everyone's nerves to shreds – including her own.

She was the daughter of Lord and Lady Bessborough and at a very early age showed a vivid, volatile nature, high spirited and fearless. But she also had a tendency to become nervous and over excited, which perhaps should have warned of things to come. She was a Ponsonby and one caustic observer at the time wrote 'the Ponsonbys are always making sensations.'

In 1805, looking prettier than anybody had ever seen her, she married William Lamb, Lord Melbourne's second son, who was extremely rich, and settled down to be a worthy wife. She tried very hard to please her husband, though it was soon obvious that they were basically incompatible. He was anchored to the earth while she was always up in the clouds. The birth of a son, named Augustus, delighted her but he was a poor sick child from the start and though she proved to be a devoted mother, he had to be taken away to be nursed.

Living out in the country, at Brocket Hall, the Hertfordshire house she dearly loved, time hung heavy on her hands. She really had nothing to do. Reading and writing letters did not get rid of her extraordinary nervous energy. Her husband, William, was a splendid man but somewhat lethargic. She tried to cure her own boredom and rouse him by flirting with other men. When her mother-in-law, Lady Melbourne, heard she had been seen with Sir Godfrey Webster, an experienced rake, and that he had given her presents, she wrote to tell her that her behaviour was 'disgusting'. After a while Caroline's riotous carrying on did become a source of some concern to the rest of her family. She admitted on one occasion 'I behaved a little wild, riding over the downs with all the officers at my heels.'

But it was not until she was nearly 30, in 1814, that she read Byron's great

Lady Caroline Lamb

poem 'Childe Harold' and declared she had to meet him. She was told he had a club foot and bit his nails. She answered 'If he is as ugly as Aesop, I must see him'.

She first set eyes on him in an admiring circle of women at Lady Jersey's ball. The impact of his physical beauty was so unexpected, she had to turn away. She refused to be introduced to him at that point, but went home to write the famous words in her diary. She also wrote 'That beautiful, pale face will be my fate.'

One day, out riding, she paid an impromptu call on Lord and Lady Holland at Holland House. She was told that Lord Byron was expected. Hot, dusty and dishevelled she protested she could not be presented to him in that

Lord Byron

state. She ran upstairs to wash and as she came down again Byron watched with mounting interest, the entrancing little figure in riding habit, eyes sparkling and gold curls, tumbled from the exercise.

'I must present Lord Byron to you,' said Lady Holland.

Bending towards Caroline he whispered: 'The offer was made to you before. Why did you resist it?'

She could certainly resist him no longer. He begged permission to call next day, then again after that. Once he brought her a rose and a carnation with the sardonic comment 'Your Ladyship, I am told, likes all that is new and rare – for a moment.' Perhaps it would have been better for him if the attraction had been fleeting.

For the next few months she was at his side all the time, everywhere. She was obviously in the throes of a passion she could not and did not care to hide. People began to ask them to parties together as if they were man and wife, but that was a result of her behaviour. Byron was always a little aloof. The Duchess of Devonshire commented tartly 'She is, as usual, doing all sorts of imprudent things for him and with him. . . .'

She kept her wildness in check because she knew he preferred tranquil women. But she poured out her adoration in letters: 'How very pale you are . . . a statue of white marble. I never see you without wishing to cry.' Her cousin reported wryly 'Lord Byron is still on his pedastal and Caroline doing homage.'

By September of that year Byron was longing to be rid of her. He felt suffocated, worn out by her clinging, obssessive attention. He was tired of being made conspicious, weary of her restless vivacity and endless chatter. She refused to let him go.

First she bombarded him with letters, in one of them assuring him that if he was in need of money all her jewels were at his service. If she met him at a party, purely by accident, she would always make sure she returned from it in his carriage and accompanied by him. This made him irritated. But even worse was her habit of waiting in the street for him if he was attending a party to which she had not been invited. One night as he left Devonshire House after a particularly grand reception she was seen to run after his carriage and stop it from leaving, her body half in and half out.

Byron still wrote to her, trying to assure her of his affection, for he was not an unkind man. But she knew now that he was trying to get away from her and all the wildness that had been kept in control for his sake broke loose.

She began to watch him endlessly, to find out where he was going, who he was going to see. She arranged for someone to spy on him at his lodgings and report back to her in detail. One day she disguised herself as a tradesman – she always looked convincingly like a young man in masculine dress – and alled round at his house at nine o'clock in the evening. Byron's valet, who did not see through the disguise, let her in to speak with him. She let her cloak fall, then threw herself at his feet. He had a very difficult time persuading her to go home.

The climax of the whole affair came when Caroline ran away. She left a house in chaos behind her and her mother, Lady Bessborough, so ill with worry she nearly had a stroke. Lord Byron found her and brought her back. She threatened that if he ever as much as stirred from London, she would do it again. It seems she had heard rumours that he was planning to return to Greece.

Lady Bessborough's pitiful condition brought on by her daughter's behaviour, was the main topic of talk among her servants. Caroline received a letter from Mrs Peterson, the housekeeper, in which she called her 'cruel and unnatural' to upset her mother so. 'Shame on you' wrote the old servant. 'You have exposed yourself to all London'. And indeed she had. People did nothing but talk about Caro Lamb and Lord Byron.

Caroline's husband was persuaded to take her for a holiday to Ireland for the sake of her health and to give everybody a bit of peace. She was pale, thin, nervous and her eyes strangely dilated. She had driven herself to the edge of madness. Even from Ireland she wrote telling him of her 'lonely, lovelorn condition. He answered: 'Amuse yourself. But leave me quiet.'

Lord Byron now made it clear to everyone that if she persisted, he would leave England. 'I shall enter into no explanations, write no epistles, nor will I meet her if it can be avoided and certainly *never* but in society.' He went to stay with Lady Oxford, but kept his whereabouts secret from Caroline. She began to suspect the truth and wrote to everyone in an attempt to find out. She did not hear from him for weeks and one day threatened to cut her throat. Lady Bessborough, the best of mothers, grasped the blade as she flourished it in the air and defied her to pull it through her hand.

There was another flurry of scandal when Caroline forged Byron's signature perfectly in order to get hold of a picture of him she desperately wanted. But worse was to come. The two of them met at Lady Heathcote's ball. They exchanged a few barbed pleasantries about Caroline dancing the waltz, then moved in to supper. Precisely what happened next goes according to whether you read Caroline's version or Byron's, but there was suddenly a knife in Caroline's hand and blood on her dress. There was some excuse about scratching herself with a piece of glass, but nobody believed it. Whether she intended just to maim herself or use it on Byron will never be known. People crowded round, took it away from her, then went on with the dancing.

Despite all that had been said Byron agreed to see Caroline once more before he left England for good. She went to his rooms in the Albany. 'Poor

Caro', he said, 'If everyone hates me, you, I see, will never change – not even with ill usage.' She answered him calmly. 'Yes, I am changed and will come near you no more.'

William Lamb, having decided to stay with Caroline, against the advice of his family, began to think how he could repair her reputation and re-establish her in society.

Unfortunately Caroline felt the urge to write. She began a novel which she called *Glenarvan*, and as though in an attempt to purge herself, finished it at breakneck speed in a fortnight and delivered it to the publishers. Its central character was obviously Byron, but in her indictment of a false society she also clearly outlined the figures of her husband, her mother-in-law and dozens of famous people she knew. The book was a bestseller. People read it avidly, identifying themselves and their friends sometimes with shock and horror at what she had revealed.

This, coming after the Byron affair nearly ruined her.

There was never anything in her life to compare with Byron. She never really recovered from her love for him. The night before he died she dreamed of him for the first time since they parted and jumped out of bed screaming.

By some stroke of fate they were to meet once more. She had been ill. On the day of her first outing her carriage was held up by a funeral cortege. It was Lord Byron's.

Unity Mitford

She would sit at Hitler's feet while he gently stroked her hair. At night before she went to sleep in a bedroom hung with swastikas, she would pray before his photograph. She thought he was the saviour of mankind, the Messiah.

For a time not even Eva Braun came as close to the Führer as Unity Mitford, the blonde English aristocrat who looked so like the embodiment of splendid Aryan womanhood that he admired and who was one of his most devoted and fanatical admirers.

As far as she was concerned Adolf Hitler could do no wrong. Even his solution to the Jewish problem was perfectly acceptable. 'They're Jews,' she would say contemptuously, 'Just Jews, and they must be got rid of.' For him there was fascination in the very fact that an upper crust English girl could so embrace the Nazi creed. He treated her with the utmost courtesy and at times, in company, referred to her as Lady Mitford.

Lord and Lady Redesdale, her parents, both eccentric and nostalgically Edwardian, had produced an astonishing crop of daughters. The Mitford girls were to become famous everywhere. But Unity was the one who took some swallowing and in the end spoiled her parents' lives.

Fate gave some strong signs of her future, right from the beginning. Her grandfather was a friend of the German composer, Wagner. When she was born on the 8 August 1914 she was given the names Unity Valkyrie, the second being that of Wotan's maiden and Wagner's great opera. She always preferred to spell it 'Walküre' in the original German form. Then Lord Redesdale bought a gold mine near Culver Park in Canada, where the family went prospecting for fun but found no fortune. It was called the Swastika Mine.

Compared with their past wealth, the Redesdales were beginning to feel the pinch. Lord Redesdale, a roaring bull of a man who could not understand anyone not like himself, such as Jews, Catholics or foreigners, made some unwise investments which dipped the family fortunes still lower. However, by the time Unity reached an impressionable age in 1926 they still had a town house at 26, Rutland Gate in London, a vast place with a ballroom and five floors of bedrooms and a house on the family estate at Swinbrook in the Cotswolds, which Lord Redesdale had designed with a cottage atmosphere in mind, but which turned out to be more like a barracks.

As Rutland Gate was usually 'let out' they led a country life at Swinbrook, each of the Mitford girls having the freedom to develop her own strikingly different character. Unity, a big, ungainly girl with fair hair chopped off in a hard fringe above baleful blue eyes, intimidated all the governesses. She could unnerve her father too. She would sit at the dinner table staring at him while he chewed mouthfuls of mashed potato, until he flew into a rage. Her mother, called Muv, sailed through it all, quietly getting on with her embroidery and good works.

By the time she was 15, Unity became bored with Swinbrook and was sent off to St Margaret's boarding school at Bushey in Hertfordshire. She was expelled a year later. When she was old enough she did the round of debutante balls and dances, dressed in the required chiffon or satin, but very soon the only garment she was to be interested in was the black shirt of the fascists.

She had become very close to her sister, Diana, in spite of the four year age gap between them. Diana, the older of the two, was deeply influenced by Oswald Mosley, leader of the British fascist movement, a dramatic looking man with black hair and an intense white face. After Mosley had been to Rome in 1932 for an audience with Mussolini, he came back determined to copy the European fascists and soon his supporters were wearing black shirts on the streets of London. Diana decided to throw in her lot with him. Unity, impressed and excited swallowed the fascist bait whole.

When Mosley visited Swinbrook to see Diana on 14 June 1933, he gave Unity the emblem from his own lapel together with a fascist salute, which she returned. She could hardly wait to sign the pledge. Proudly wearing Mosley's emblem on her coat, she strode into party headquarters in Lower Grosvenor Place, London five days later to tell them she wanted to join. She was given a frosty reception. They had had enough of frivolous society girls, attracted by the uniform. She had made a mistake. Next time her approach was more respectful. She drove from Swinbrook into Oxford to the local branch of the British Union of Fascists where she was eyed sceptically by a roomful of blackshirts. She told them she knew Mosley personally and had read his book. Vincent Keens, a 30-year-old Canadian, who was the Oxford leader listened to her for a while and was amazed. This was the genuine upper crust article all right. And she was serious. He handed her the membership card and she was sworn in.

People began to duck out of the way when they saw her coming. She wore the swastika, signed herself with the swastika and talked continually about Hitler. Worst of all was her increasing fanaticism about the Jews. One day, out shopping with a friend she suggested popping into Selfridge's to make a record of their own voices, just for fun. The friend made her contribution to the disc then was appalled to hear Unity chanting 'The Yids, the Yids, we've got to get rid of the Yids' – the standard cry of the blackshirts as they marched through the streets of London.

She enrolled at London County Council's School of Art in the Spring of 1933 but only stayed long enough to be able to call herself an art student. Far more momentous things were happening.

In August that year the Nazis staged their first Nuremberg Rally, a colossal, frightening expression of power in which 400,000 party members, including members of the dreaded ss and Hitler Youth saluted their leader. Unity was chosen as one of the BUF representatives to go to Nuremberg. She gloried in every minute of it. For the first time she saw Hitler, heard his voice. 'From that moment I knew there was no one else in the world I would rather meet.' she said. The official Nazi brochure published after the rally, has a photograph of Unity in a tweed suit with her black shirt, her black gloved hand held up in salute – the only woman in the British delegation.

Some time in the spring of 1934 she told her parents that she would like to live most of the time in Germany. They sent her to a finishing school run by a

Unity Mitford

Baroness Laroche, a haunt for upper class English girls in Munich before the war, where they were taught the German language, painting, piano, singing and how to look the other way to avoid endangering their own lives. In other words if they saw a scuffle and suspected it was a Jew being beaten or harrassed, they should avert their eyes and hurry by. Unity was heard to say 'Jolly good. Serves them right. We should go and cheer.'

Baroness Laroche began to feel that Miss Mitford was an alarming pupil. The school was not very big and she seemed to fill it with her overpowering fervour for the Nazis and their leader. She was constantly singing the Horst Wessel Lied and other Nazi songs, had portraits of Hitler on her bedroom wall and would sometimes bring ss men back to the house, much to the Baroness' horror. Wearing her black shirt and black leather gauntlet gloves, Unity took part in torchlight processions and attended every ceremony and reception where she knew Hitler would make his appearance.

She was determined to meet him, but had no intention of joining the thousands of women who threw themselves at Hitler's feet, who moaned and fainted and sometimes even swallowed the gravel upon which he had walked. She had a better way.

Hitler's favourite restaurant was the Osteria Bavaria in Munich. He went there often, with two or three others, quite informally dressed in a raincoat holding his favourite Alsatian dog with one hand and a whip with the other. Unity took the same table every day and waited to see him arrive. At last he became curious about the attractive blonde who seemed to turn up everywhere and one day sent an aide to her table asking if she would join him for lunch.

It was the beginning of their remarkable relationship.

David Pryce Jones, who went to see Albert Speer, Hitler's Minister of Armaments, when he was writing his biography of Unity Mitford quotes him as saying 'She was highly in love with him, we could see it easily. Her face brightened up, her eyes gleaming, staring at Hitler ... and possibly Hitler liked to be admired by this young woman, she was quite attractive – even if nothing happened he was excited by the possibility of a love affair with her.'

But Unity Mitford herself described Hitler as a celibate man and it is not considered likely that she ever became his mistress. Her attraction, for him, was something quite different. To start with, she was an aristocrat and educated to be a lady. She addressed him adoringly as Mein Führer and talked to him about art, literature, music, dogs, travel, in a lively and interesting way. He enjoyed her company.

Before long she was seen in his entourage on every big occasion and she was invited to join him on many informal outings at which he was always an exemplary host. He seemed to be very fond of asking people for tea. She would receive a call instructing her to be at the Chancellory by four o'clock and would find he had bought mountains of cream buns which she was expected to eat, though he only nibbled a dry cracker. She was never alone with him, however. There would always be others present.

Lord and Lady Redesdale, bewildered by what was happening, went out to Munich in the winter of 1934-5 to find their daughter had turned into a full fledged Nazi maiden. She introduced them to Hitler. Later she tried to draw them even more into her German life and succeeded to a certain extent, though they never got over the tragedy which her life was leading up to.

Some of those close to Hitler felt that her constant presence was a nuisance. Obviously convinced she was not an agent, he would talk about party politics and far reaching policy while she was there. Goebbles, the womaniser, liked her but thought that her intensity did more harm than good to the cause. Unity became close friends with Goebbels' wife, Magda, and would sometimes stay with the family for weekends. If there was a big party at the Chancellory in Berlin, Hitler would ask Frau Goebbels to invite Unity to stay the night.

Her own favourite among the Nazis was Julius Streicher, the Jew baiter and torturer. It was to hear him that she attended one of those Nazi get togethers that turned out to be so sinister. They were all gathered in the pretty, rolling countryside at Hesselberg for a weekend of bread and circuses. Plump party members in Leder hosen and swastika armbands swilled down gallons of beer and fair-haired Nazi maidens twined flowers in their hair. Streicher spoke to them at ten at night, his voice ringing out in the darkness, telling them to be revenged on the Jews 'who after the last war had tried to make an end to the German race.'

'The English are ready for peace' he yelled 'It is the Jew who does not want peace'. Unity, blue eyes shining, fair hair drawn back from her face was called by him to the microphone and she affirmed her solidarity with the German people and with the struggle of Julius Streicher.

After that people began to be very wary of her. It was not safe, they realized, to criticise anyone in her hearing. People had been known to be arrested 48 hours after being in her company. Once she boasted that it was such fun to have supper with Streicher as he'd have the Jews in after a meal and make them eat grass to amuse his guests. She was obviously setting out to shock people, especially the English women still left in Berlin and Munich, for they loathed her.

Hitler invited both Unity and her sister, Diana, who had just married Mosley secretly in Germany, to attend the 1936 Olympic games. These games, planned on a Roman scale, were intended to show the world that the Nazi party had reached its zenith. Hitler, a solitary figure in an aura of blue white light projected by 180 search lights, had never seemed as hypnotic to the awestruck Unity. But Hitler had played a trick on her that took the glory out of the proceedings. He had given her a ticket in the reserved stand next to Eva Braun. The two women, deeply jealous of each other, did not bother to hide their mutual dislike. Eva Braun had been known to say of Unity 'She is known as the Walküre and looks the part, including her legs. I know these are the dimension he prefers but . . . .!'

She was home for Christmas 1936 and for the final spasm of the abdication crisis. She went to the House of Lords to hear the abdication speech read and commented 'Hitler will be terribly unhappy about it. He wanted Edward to stay as King.'

Back in Germany she was happy to be able to sit at Hitler's feet while he talked. They used to flip through the pages of *The Tatler* together and mark the names of those people who might come over to them when he occupied England. He showed an unusually light side of his nature by imitating Mussolini and Goering and other top Nazis. Sometimes he even imitated himself – and Neville Chamberlain, then British Prime Minister.

Some of the German hierarchy began to question just what Unity Mitford wanted. Did she have an assignment from the Secret Service? Was she an agent? In the end they used a word for her which implied she was a fellow traveller. Ribbentrop disliked her, so did Rudolf Hess, who was jealous as well as suspicious.

Wild stories began to circulate about Hitler asking her to marry him. Unity was angry because she knew it was out of the question and she was afraid that he might think the rumours had been inspired by her. Lord Redesdale did what he could to put an end to it. A statement by him appeared in the Sunday Pictorial: 'There is not, nor has there ever been any question of an engagement between my daughter and Herr Hitler. The Führer lives only for his country and has no time for marriage.'

Home for another visit she was given a roasting by the press and had a taste of British feeling which shook her more than she liked to admit. With a small group of BUF members she attended a Labour party rally in Hyde Park protesting at non intervention in the Spanish Civil War. They stationed themselves beside Sir Stafford Cripps, hoisted the swastika banner and gave the fascist salute. She had not said anything but someone recognized her. Her badge was ripped off and thrown away and she was surrounded by a crowd of men and women who threatened to chuck her in the Serpentine. Three police officers arrived to escort her away but she was kicked and some people tried to follow her on to a bus.

She felt it was time for her to to go back to Germany and stay there. But the sands were running out and things would never be the same again.

Hitler's march into Austria in the spring of 1938 and the signing of the Anschluss thrilled Unity. He had given her an invitation to join him in the victory celebrations at the Imperial Hotel in Vienna. But to her great disappointment, she only saw him for a few minutes.

By the end of May Hitler was in a rage with Czechoslovakia and threatening to crush the state that had dared to partially mobilise its army because of his sinister troop movements. Unity set off for Prague and stayed at the Esplanade Hotel. She wore the swastika provocatively and was asked by the Czech government to leave as these were sensitive times. But she set off instead for Carlsbad and was arrested en route. When a representative of the British legation arrived to help he was told bluntly that she was a Nazi and had been warned at several road blocks not to drive through. She was asking for trouble, and had got it. In her luggage they found a Nazi dagger and a portrait of Hitler. She promised to leave immediately. On her return she told how she had been 'revoltingly molested' in Prague.

By the summer of 1938 Unity found it was not possible to see Hitler in the old informal way. She had to wait for an invitation and would then be conducted to his table by an aide. He was always pleased to see her and greeted her, even when surrounded by his top men, with great affability. When she attended the Nuremberg rally in September, taking her parents who had been converted by her, she found Hitler grave and preoccupied.

For the next twelve months, while Europe slid from peace to war, she divided her time between Germany and England. The Führer had offered her a flat from a number that were to become empty in the Agnesstrasse. She went along to find they were owned by Jews who had been warned to remove their belongings and whose tragic fate was only too obvious. Behaving as though they were faceless, without identity, not even there, she went about brightly making her selection. She had been thoroughly indoctrinated by the Nazi creed.

When her flat was finished it was very colourful, very chic, with deep pile carpets. The whole thing was a present from Hitler. Behind her bed hung two great swastika flags, their ends draped over the pillows and by her bedside the inevitable photograph of the Führer. In her sitting room was a writing table, one drawer of which contained a revolver. 'When I'm obliged to quit Germany' she told a friend 'I'll kill myself'.

She never thought England would stand firm. She began listening to all the news bulletins and heard Lord Halifax, the foreign secretary, pledging support for Poland should Hitler invade, in accordance with the repeated pledge to do so.

Distraught, she went to the British Consul for news. He told her that all British nationals were leaving and he advised her to go home too. 'I don't contemplate it' she answered. 'Then', answered the Consul, 'you no longer have the protection of Great Britain'. Always determined to have the last word Unity flung back 'I have the much better protection of the Führer.'

By 29 August she was listening to every news bulletin on her radio. She could not believe what was happening. The thought of a war between Germany and Great Britain was more than she could stand.

On the morning of 3 September when war was declared she locked her flat, got into her car and drove to the Ministry of the Interior. She handed in a heavy envelope which was found to contain all her badges and emblems and a farewell letter to Hitler.

Unity on her return to England

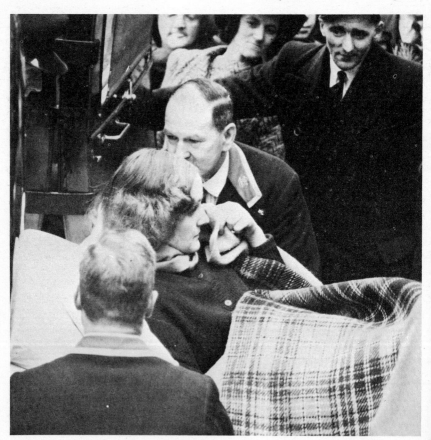

A few hours later the police discovered a young fair haired woman slumped on a seat in the English Garden. She had shot herself in the temple, but was still alive.

It was some hours before she was recognized as Unity Mitford by doctors in the Munich clinic to which she had been taken. Hitler was informed immediately. He instructed the clinic to do all they could to save her. He would pay for everything.

At first her case seemed hopeless. The bullet had lodged in her head and any operation to remove it would probably cause brain damage. After long consultations it was decided to leave the bullet where it was. At first she could not speak properly, then refused to admit she had shot herself 'I had such a terrible fall' she would say.

Hitler went to visit her at the clinic on 8 November, taking sheaves of flowers. It was the last time she was to see him. He was deeply shaken by the change in her and when she told him she would like to go back to England, he made no objection. He not only set the wheels in motion for her return but gave instructions that her parents were to be allowed into the country to fetch her.

Her arrival home was a nine day wonder. Too many other things were happening. There was some talk about why wasn't she interned as a traitor but Herbert Morrison, the Home Secretary, said that in her present condition, she was no threat to security.

The old Valkyrie was no more. Unity Mitford was now a quiet, slightly odd young woman with a bit of an obsession for kind clergymen. She went to church regularly but became increasingly lonely in spite of the efforts of her family. Her parents had parted, so after the war, Lady Redesdale decided to take her daughter to live on the tranquil island of Inchkenneth off the coast of Mull. She had a good life there until the old wound began to make itself felt. Though outwardly fit she began to need special nursing. On 28 May, 1948 she became very ill and was taken by boat to the little West Highland Cottage Hospital in Oban. She was past help and died from meningitis caused by a cerebral abcess brought on by the festering bullet. Such a quiet end for one of Wotan's maidens.

Chapter Six

Witchery

Most people think of dark deeds and equally dark women when they talk of witchcraft. Thousands have been labelled witches through the centuries but a few stand out as especially sinister figures....

Alice Kyteler

In the dusty, mouldering pages of some 14th century archives lies the story of a beautiful woman, rich, influential, probably of Anglo Norman stock. She lived in the town of Kilkenny in Ireland where, it was recorded, she had been married to three wealthy husbands in succession and in the year 1324 was about to lose her fourth. Her name was Lady Alice Kyteler and she was one of the most sinister figures of her time.

Lady Alice was not popular with her neighbours partly because of her inordinate wealth, partly because of her arrogance and haughty, overbearing manner.

There were also rumours that her Ladyship was involved in the practice of witchcraft and sorcery, though no one could prove it.

Her first husband had been one William Outlawe, a banker and money lender who died before 1302. Then she married Adam le Blund of Callan who expired by 1311 to be followed by Richard de Valle who also went to his maker rather quickly.

Two of these husbands had been widowers with children who lost their inheritance when the besotted fellows left everything to Lady Alice. If they suspected foul play, they said nothing at the time.

However, when Lady Alice's fourth and latest husband, Sir John le Poer fell dangerously ill in 1324 with a wasting disease which made his nails fall from his fingers and toes and caused his hair to come out in handfuls, the children began to hint that their fathers had died from equally strange illnesses with similar symptoms.

Sir John, in love with his wife, did not want to hear what they were implying. But when one of his maid servants began to give such broad hints that it would have been foolish to ignore her, Sir John decided it was time for him to act.

He demanded his wife's key to her room. When she refused he seized her and after a struggle, wrenched it from her belt. A search soon brought to light a number of boxes and chests, all heavily padlocked. Forcing them open the wretched man found inside all the evidence he needed to prove that his wife was a poisoner and deeply involved in witchcraft.

Sir John gathered together all the strange powders, phials and potions, the wicked looking instruments and wafers of sacramental bread inscribed with the name of Satan and sent them, in the safekeeping of two monks, to the Bishop of Ossory, whose diocese it was. The Bishop was to prove a formidable prosecutor.

He was an English Franciscan named Richard De Ledrede, known to be a fanatic in hunting out those who dabbled in sorcery and a man greedy for funds. Should Lady Alice be found guilty her wealth would be confiscated by the church.

After an investigation the Bishop accused her of being involved in 'divers kinds of witchcraft' and ordered her arrest along with eleven accomplices including her own son William Outlawe and her personal maid, Petronilla de Meath.

The Bishop's indictment contained no fewer than seven formidable charges to which the inhabitants of Kilkenny listened with fascinated horror. Lady Alice, it emerged, had crept from her home in the dead of night to hold meetings with her accomplices in local churches where religious ceremonies were mocked and appalling rites performed. Living animals were sacrificed to the devil then, torn limb from limb, scattered at the cross roads. She had been expert in making charms and ointments from such hideous ingredients as the hair of criminals who had been hanged, nails from dead men's fingers, the intestines of animals, worms, poisonous herbs and flesh of babies who had died unbaptised.

All these things she was said to have boiled together in the skull of a robber who had been beheaded.

The indictment also included 'an unholy and obscure association' between Lady Alice and a demon called Robert Artisson who was described as her familiar and who would appear sometimes in the shape of a huge cat, at others like a shaggy beast or yet again in the disguise of a black prince with two tall companions, each carrying a rod in his hand. Lady Alice was said by her maid to have had sexual intercourse with this 'apparition'. Who was this creature?

Under the influence of witchcraft he was believed to be supernatural but in fact he was probably a fellow practitioner from another town or village. The Bishop cast his net wide to try to trap him, but he never succeeded. It was rumoured he must have been an educated man or a noble for no peasant would have had the wit or resource to have escaped Ossory's Inquisition for long.

That she had used her potions to kill her former husbands and to bring Sir John to the point of death was soon obvious. She had an insatiable greed for money. Her only true allegiance was to her favourite son, William Outlawe, who had proved a willing disciple in her diabolical craft. She used to perform a rite which was meant to make him rich. She would take a broom out into the streets of Kilkenny at sunset and raking all the dirt and dust towards the door of her son's house chant:

> 'To the house of William my son
> Hie all the wealth of Kilkenny town!'

It was one thing for the Bishop to order Lady Alice's arrest, quite another to take her into custody. He found himself obstructed on every side. Up to this time sorcery had been a secular crime, not under the jurisdiction of the Church so the Bishop had to ask the Lord Chancellor of Ireland to issue a writ for the arrest of the accused.

Unfortunately, the Chancellor was one Roger Outlawe, a kinsman by her first marriage who supported her.

Taking the law into his own hands, the Bishop sent two representatives to call her in person before the court of the Bishopric. She refused to accept his jurisdiction. The ecclesiastical court, she said, was not empowered to judge her or anyone else on a matter of this kind. Nevertheless, the court sat and the Bishop excommunicated her.

Her supporters took revenge by making him a prisoner in Kilkenny Castle for eighteen days and while he fretted and fumed the accused coolly indicted *him* in a secular court for defamation of character.

All this only served to stiffen the Bishop's resolve to get 'the Kyteler' in the end. Time after time he was asked to leave secular courts where he demanded her arrest. When at last, after being obstructed at every turn, permission came to bring the accused sorcerers to trial in an ecclesistical court, it was too late. The bird had flown. Helped by fellow aristocrats, the Lady Alice had gathered up her jewels and escaped to England where she lived for the rest of her days.

Her fellow witches were left to face the fire. Bishop Ossory found an ally in Lady Alice's husband, Sir John, who helped him to arrest William Outlawe. This gentleman begged to be reconciled with the church and pardon was granted him as long as he fulfilled certain penances and paid for the re-roofing of St Mary's Cathedral in Kilkenny.

Lady Alice's maid, Petronilla de Meath, eventually brought to trial with the other accomplices paid the greatest price. She was the first witch to be burned in Ireland. Yet, she declared, compared with Lady Alice she was a mere novice. Her mistress had taught her everything. She believed there was no more powerful witch in the world than her Ladyship, Alice Kyteler. The abandoned and unrepentant Petronilla went to the stake and was burned on 3 November 1324.

Lady Alice was tried and found guilty 'in absentia', but she remained safe as long as she stayed away from Ireland. The Kyteler case nevertheless became something of a landmark, not only because it was the first trial of its kind in Ireland.

The dusty, 14th century records also showed that by her instruction and teaching Lady Alice Kyteler had set out the complete witch creed for centuries to come.

La Voisin

Queen of all the witches in France during the reign of the Sun King, Louis XIV, was a woman called Catherine Deshayes Voisin, better known simply as La Voisin.

Some of the most famous and dazzling women of the day, Madame de Montespan, the King's mistress, among them, were known to have sought her help through the black arts. She thought herself invincible as she dabbled in wickedness. 'Nothing is impossible to me' she told one of her clients. 'Only another god can understand my power.'

Only when the miasma of her dark deeds threatened to touch the King himself was she brought to justice in a great purge which swept up half the witches in Paris and aired a great many scandals at high level.

La Voisin was a short, plump woman, not unattractive apart from her eyes which were piercing, like those of a bird of prey. She was said to have inherited her powers from her mother who practised as a sorceress and was so famous that even the Emperor of Austria and the King of England had asked her advice.

She lived in a neat, secluded villa in the Paris suburb of St Denis and claimed that her occupation was most innocent. 'I am a practitioner of chiromancy, a student of physiognomy' she would boast. She was indeed an uncanny fortune teller, skilled at crystal gazing, reading the Tarot cards, reading palms and reading faces. 'The lines on a face are far easier to read than the lines of the hand', she would say. 'Passion and anxiety are difficult to conceal.'

She made up love potions and happiness powders and sold them in silk and taffeta pouches, prescribed herbs for unwanted pregnancies and supplied aphrodisiacs for lagging lovers or husbands. When challenged with far worse things she had the gall to say 'I rendered an account of my arts to the Vicars General of Paris and to several doctors at the Sorbonne, to whom I had been sent for questioning, and they found nothing to criticise.' She had indeed been to the Sorbonne to discuss astrology with some of the professors and had paid a social call on the rector of the University of Paris. She even attended early mass at her parish church.

How she must have laughed for she was queen of the most powerful coven of witches in Paris and dedicated to evil. Only her enemy, La Bosse, could be compared with her. At first she had sought her clients among the common people but as her fame as a sorceress spread so did her ambition. She was brought into contact with high society and the court. Moral restraints, she found, did not matter greatly to the very rich. Men and women of great eminence would pay anything to get rid of an unwanted partner, to eliminate a rival or ensure the continuance of their power.

Poison was her speciality. She had secured the services of two women who were capable of genius when it came to making up prescriptions. They provided La Voisin with 57 different poisons from which she could improvise in hundreds of ways. By varying the fatal doses she gave to clients she was sure that the symptoms would be different. This meant that no one could establish a pattern of death and trace the poison back to her.

Curiously enough, she had made several attempts to finish off her own husband, a bankrupt jewel merchant, as she had taken as her lover an infamous criminal character calling himself Le Sage, but each time she failed. He had an ally and protector in La Voisin's maid, Margot. The poisoned dishes were usually served up to him at the family table. Once Margot saved him by jogging his elbow just as he raised a lethal bowl of soup to his lips. Another time she gave him a counter poison which worked well enough but left him with incurable hiccups and a bleeding nose. It was a great joke in La Voisin's circle of intimates. 'Bonjour Madame', they would greet her. How is your husband? Not dead yet?'

The most shocking and replusive aspect of what went on in the demure villa at St Denis was in the saying of Black Mass for which she provided priest, altar, vestments and sacrifice. For these ceremonies and séances she wore a dramatic vestment specially designed and woven for her which included a vast cloak of crimson velvet elaborately embroidered with the double head and wing spread of golden eagles. The same motif was stitched in pure gold thread on her slippers. She admitted at her trial that she had a furnace in the garden where she had disposed of the tiny corpses of hundreds of infants or embryos, aborted, premature, still-born and new born, that had been used in the Black Mass. She scattered their ashes on her garden.

It was in 1679 that Louvois, the King's Minister of War sent him a secret message saying that the woman called La Voisin had started to talk too much. She had said openly that Madame De Vivonne and Madame de la Mothe had come to her for something to do away with their husbands. Who would be talked of next? The whole court was in a stew while the King insisted that someone must get to the bottom of this poisons affair, regardless of rank, sex or position.

The name that had shocked him was that of Madame de Vivonne, sister-in-law to Madame de Montespan, who was in the intimate circle around him at court.

La Voisin, with her accomplices, was arrested with scores of others in the

Madam de Montespan

La Voisin

great purge of his capital which the King demanded. Le Sage, who had been supplanted in La Voisin's bed by a man named Latour, betrayed all her secrets. Many names were mentioned of the aristocrats involved, but La Voisin kept silent about Madame de Montespan and any services she had rendered her. It was Le Sage who blurted out her name under brutal interrogation, telling how the King's mistress had come to La Voisin for help when she thought she was losing his love. Apart from the potions given her to stimulate the King's interest, she had also taken part in the Black Mass.

The police chief, Nicolas de la Reynie, alarmed by what was emerging reported to the King. Louis ordered that any documents mentioning Madame de Montespan should be delivered to him personally. He burned the incriminating evidence with his own hand and hardly spoke to the lady again. But the police had copies and the evidence survived.

In a last minute attempt to save herself La Voisin protested that the only drugs to be found in her house were purgatives for the personal use of her family. As for the small furnace or oven in the garden, concealed by a tapestry, she said it was for baking her pâtés.

But when the police broke in they found what amounted to a small factory for making poisons, copies of the Luciferian Credo, a store of black candles and incense and a collection of wax figurines bristling with needles and pins.

La Voisin protested in vain. She was burned alive for her sins. Unrepentant to the last, she repelled the crucifix held in front of her as the flames climbed higher.

Chapter
Seven

Queens of Crime

Poison is always said to be the most popular form of murder by the female sex. Simple, clean, it can be administered over a cosy cup of tea. Some women however have chosen to make their mark on criminal history in other ways. . . .

Amelia Dyer

Her name was used, like that of the bogeyman, to scare young children into being good. If you don't behave, Victorian parents would say, you'll go and stay with Amelia Dyer. And everyone knew what that meant. It meant you didn't come back.

Amelia Dyer was a 'baby farmer' who, when finally charged with her appalling crimes, was discovered to be a monster who had been quietly killing off unwanted infants for a period of about 20 years.

She was originally a Bristol woman who had been born, brought up and married in that city. Short and squat, with a well-scrubbed look, her hair dragged into a bun at the back of her head, she belonged to the Salvation Army and went out at weekends to sing hymns on draughty street corners. Her husband worked in a vinegar factory.

When the Dyers split up, about the year 1875, she found it necessary to earn money to keep herself and her daughter, Polly. Rather than take in washing, she became the local midwife, occasionally fostering those she brought into the world. But, she discovered, far more lucrative than midwifery or casually looking after children for whom she might, or might not, get paid, was the business of baby farming. This was a practice that sprang up towards the end of the last century. It was considered illegal, but thrived nevertheless. Mothers with unwanted or inconvenient infants farmed them out to working-class women sometimes for a few months, sometimes for years. The women were suitably paid at the start, then left alone to get on with the job. Sometimes, the real mother never came back.

Amelia Dyer realized she could earn a reasonable living if she was clever about it. The more babies she 'farmed' the more money she would earn. Her problem would be, how to accomodate them all, how to make room. . . . .

She started a baby farm at her cottage in the village of Long Ashton, south west of Bristol, but eventually she was discovered and jailed for six weeks. After that she fell on bad times, was taken into the workhouse at Barton Regis and did not leave again until June 1895.

She left the workhouse with an old crone called Granny Smith and the pair of them went to live in Cardiff with Amelia's daughter, Polly, now married. It must have been a wretched household. Polly's husband, Arthur, was unemployed; they had a baby that died of convulsions, and there was no money.

Soon it became necessary to get out of the way of creditors and the police so

he entire household packed up its belongings on an old cart and took to the
oad. They came eventually to the village of Caversham, outside Reading
nd took a cottage there in Piggott's Road.

Amelia Dyer decided to go back to her old business, using a false name. She
nserted an advertisement in the local paper: 'Couple having no child would
ke the care of one or would adopt one. Terms £10' and made it known by
vord of mouth that the house was open for boarders.

First to arrive was the ten-month-old baby daughter of a barmaid, then
ame a nine-year-old boy, Willie Thornton, followed by another baby and a
irl of four. Amelia was also paid £10 by a woman called Eleanor Marmon,
vho asked her to take care of her illegitimate daughter, Doris. A baby boy,
Iarry Simmons, was received from a lady whose maid had given birth to
im, then disappeared.

Amelia took them all into her loving care. But on 30 March 1896
argemen working on the river Thames near Reading fished a brown paper
arcel out of the water. To their horror they found it contained the body of a
aby girl, strangled with tape, and a brick used to weigh her down. Then on
 April two more parcels, this time in a carpet bag, were dragged out of the
vater. They contained the tiny bodies of Doris Marmon and Harry Simmons,
vho had also been strangled with tape.

The police made a discovery that led them straight to the murderer. On
ne of the pieces of brown paper they could just decipher the address 'Mrs
Thomas, Piggott's Road, Lower Caversham'. Two days later, having
dentified Mrs Thomas as Amelia Dyer, they arrested her.

There was pandemonium when she was taken to the police station. First
he tried to kill herself with a pair of scissors then, that having failed she tried
o throttle herself with a bootlace. Both her daughter, Polly, and her son-in-
aw, Arthur, were also taken in.

Police continued dragging the river and found four more of Amelia Dyer's
iny victims, bringing the number to seven. She never revealed how many she
ad killed altogether but it was known that at the time of her arrest she was
till taking payment for infants long dead. She said, without emotion 'you'll
ecognize mine by the tape.'

While in prison she did try to save her daughter and son-in-law and clear
hem from suspicion by writing a letter to the Superintendant of Police. 'I do
nost solemnly swear that neither of them had anything to do with it' she
vrote. 'They never knew I contemplated doing such a wicked thing until too
ate.' As it happened, Polly, the daughter she loved, became chief witness for
he prosecution, giving evidence against her mother both at the magistrates
earing and later at the Old Bailey.

Amelia Dyer was charged with the murder of Doris Marmon and tried before Mr Justice Hawkins on 21 and 22 May 1896. Polly described how her mother had turned up at her home in Willesden carrying a ham and a carpet bag and holding the baby girl, Doris Marmon, whom she said she was looking after temporarily for a neighbour. It was cold and Polly sat her mother down by the fire in the kitchen while she went out to fetch more coal. When she came back, the baby had disappeared, and her mother was pushing the battered old carpet bag under the sofa. That night she insisted on sleeping on the sofa. By next morning Harold Simmons, a baby Polly was minding for her mother, had also disappeared. She was puzzled, but didn't know what to do. Later that day, the Palmers took her to Paddington station to catch the Reading train. While she went to buy some cakes to eat on the journey, her son-in-law held the carpet bag, remarking on how heavy it was. It was of course the same carpet bag she later dumped in the Thames with the two tiny strangled corpses huddled inside.

Her defence lawyer, a Mr Kapadia, accepted that she was guilty – she had in fact never denied her actions – but that she was insane. There was much argument and contention over this point, but the jury took just five minutes to find her 'Guilty' but 'Not insane.' For had she not kept a careful list of those she fostered and an even more careful list of the money paid to her, often long after the babies were dead.

She was hanged at Newgate Prison on 10 June 1896 leaving a letter stating 'What was done I did do myself' and regretting the trouble she had brought on her daughter.

But Amelia Dyer's trial achieved something. It brought about a sharp decline in the practice of baby farming. For who knew whether there might be another Mrs Dyer, waiting to earn an honest £10?

Frances Howard

As a family the Howards were a violent crowd, full of valour in wartime, full of passion in peace. But few of them had as little respect for human life as the bewitching Frances, one of the great beauties at the court of James I.

Their lineage was ancient and powerful, dating back to William the Conqueror and Lord Howard of Effingham who improved their image by defeating the Armada in 1588. But throughout history they had also been famous for a record of intrigue and plotting, violent temper and greed that made all men wary of them. They had managed to stay in power and royal favour by sheer skill.

Frances was the daughter of Lord Thomas Howard, created Earl of Suffolk when James I came to the throne in 1603. He was an unscrupulous man whose career ended in disgrace when he was accused of gross embezzlement of public funds. Her mother was no less greedy. She was born and brought up at the family's country seat at Audley End, near Saffron Walden and for a time her charm and sweet face hid her true character. It was her father's uncle, the Earl of Northampton, who detected the embryo of something evil and, with devilish cunning began to wield a sinister influence over her.

She was married at fifteen to Robert Devereux, Earl of Essex, but the young couple were separated almost at once as the King, who had taken the handsome boy under his wing, insisted that Robert return to Oxford to finish his degree, then join the army abroad.

This left Frances free to practice her powers of seduction at Court as Countess of Essex, and she used them to great advantage. Her first affair was with the Prince of Wales but his attractions paled to nothing once she set eyes on the King's favourite, the darkly handsome Robert Carr, Viscount Rochester, a Scot who had come to England on the accession of James I.

Lord Northampton, aware of her passion and thinking to further his own interests, brought them together. Though Rochester was at first wary of becoming involved because of the King's affection for the absent Devereux, he soon succumbed to the advances of this most seductive woman.

He insisted their intrigue must be carried on away from the eyes of the Court. But he had one disadvantage. He was not an educated man and had no skill in writing love letters. He realized he needed an accomplice, a go-between who would also write the letters for him. The man he chose was Thomas Overbury, son of Sir Nicholas Overbury of Bourton on the Hill in Gloucestershire. Rochester had first met him in Edinburgh when he himself was page to the Earl of Dunbar. They became inseparable friends and travelled south together to join James's Court. The arrangement was successful and for a time the lovers had no cause for alarm.

The first cloud came on their horizon with the return of Essex, who was eager to sample the joys of married life with his beautiful, 18-year-old wife. At first she pretended to be timid. When he became more pressing she was frigid. Though they occupied the same bed and the same room she would not yield. She cared only for Rochester and any other man repulsed her. Desperately, the Earl asked her father 'to remind his daughter of her obedience as a wife'. But a father can do little in such circumstances. The stalemate lasted until

Essex was struck down with smallpox and was too ill to bother about his wife.

This gave Frances time to scheme. She had two objects: to kill her husband's natural desire for her and to inflame Rochester's passion still further. She decided the only effective course would be through witchcraft. She was given, in utter secrecy, the address of a Mrs Anne Turner, widow of a doctor of physic in London who apparantly worked hand in glove with the sinister and infamous Dr Simon Forman. At night she paid a visit to their 'surgery' and was prescribed evil looking potions and powders which were guaranteed to be effective.

When Essex recovered his health and strength and began to act like a normal husband she started to administer her poison. After a few doses he should have been utterly debilitated, but there was no effect. However strong she made the potion, he remained lusty, hale and hearty. Sending a note to Mrs Turner, with instructions to burn it after she had read it (the instructions were never carried out) she begged frantically for a more effective remedy. She wrote the damning words 'I cannot be happy as long as this man liveth'. She had also, it emerged later, consulted a Norfolk witch called Mary Woods who swore she had received a diamond ring and a promise of £1,000 if she could produce a poison that would dispatch Essex within three or four days.

At court Rochester was now at the height of his power, and Frances watched jealously as he moved freely among the beautiful women who sought his favour. She was even more incensed as she realized that her lover was anxious not to jeopardise his favourable position by associating too openly with her. She resorted again to spells and potions and even took part in black magic ceremonies. The repulsive Dr Forman made wax figures of Frances and Rochester in the act of love.

Whatever the reason, Rochester seemed to be drawn more and more towards her, eventually declaring he could not live without her. The lovers met whenever they could either at Mrs Turner's lodgings in Hammersmith or at a house in Hounslow which Frances had bought specially for the purpose. Their meetings were known to only one other person and that was Thomas Overbury, who had now been knighted for his loyalty, Rochester having told the King what a staunch friend he was.

Overbury did not like what was happening. He did not like Frances. He saw her as a vicious woman whose evil practices would bring down his friend. When he heard that she was determined to seek a divorce from her husband in order to marry Rochester he could hold his tongue no longer. 'If you do marry that filthy, base woman you will utterly ruin your honour and yourself; you shall never do it by my advice or consent' he blurted out to the man he loved and admired more than any other. But Rochester was blinded by his infatuation and the relationship between the two men was never the same.

Frances Howard

Frances heard what had happened, heard that Overbury was talking about her openly at court and with hatred vowed she would destroy him. The King had already shown some sympathy for her divorce. If he discovered she was not the virtuous woman he thought, he might change his mind. From that moment Overbury's death was certain.

She turned to her old mentor, Lord Northampton for help. He was jealous of Rochester's influence as the King's favourite and was only too anxious to work against him, whatever the reason. Together they set out to poison Rochester's mind against his friend, making great capital out of their insinuation that Overbury was plotting to step into his shoes and was already being shown great favour by the King.

Poison was also poured into the royal ear so that when Overbury refused James's offer to send him as Ambassador to the Low Countries, the King suspected him of ulterior motives and sent him to the Tower for 'a matter of high contempt'.

Frances was going to make sure he never came out alive. She paid an agent called Weston to work for her, and managed to get him a position in the Tower, eventually arranging for him to become personal assistant to the wretched Overbury. It would be his task to administer the poison to the prisoner's food, making sure that nothing was left on the plate as evidence.

The first attempt to poison Sir Thomas failed because Weston was caught red handed by Sir Gervase Elwes, Lieutenant of the Tower. After some thought Elwes decided to keep silent. For all he knew Weston might be acting on instructions from the highest level and he did not want to make life difficult for himself. But he was a humane man and did not intend to let Overbury be poisoned if he could help it. He must have intercepted most of the jellies and tarts, cold meats and sauces that Frances sent in for him. They contained so much poison that had he eaten them he would have had enough in his system to kill 20 men. Frances had paid Mrs Turner and an apothecary James Franklin, to supply her with seven different poisons. That none of them had worked seemed unexplicable, unless she was being cheated. When a rumour began to circulate that Overbury was due to be released from the Tower, she got rid of the useless Weston. She took an immense risk. With Northumberland, she contacted a young man called William Reeve, assistant to Dr Paul de Lobell, the French physician who was attending prisoners in the Tower. For £20 reward Reeve stole from his master a solution of mercury sublimate. It was given to Sir Thomas Overbury as a medicine. He swallowed it without any suspicion and died in agony.

Frances had already petitioned for divorce from the Earl of Essex and on 16 May 1613 a commission was at last appointed to examine her claim that her marriage was null and void, because her husband was impotent. Essex denied this emphatically and people were inclined to believe his side of the story. However, after some interference on the part of the King, who found the whole thing distasteful, nullity was declared. The pair of them were free to start again. Essex had no idea at the time how lucky he had been to escape with his life.

The marriage between Rochester, now created Earl of Somerset and Frances Essex took place towards the end of that year, the bride radiant in white with her long fair hair flowing loosely down her back as a symbol of purity and innocence. The whole court attended with the King and Queen and a great deal of money was spent on the occasion.

Rochester still had no idea that he had married a murderess.

But if Frances thought she could now settle down happily with the man who had obsessed her and dominated her passions and emotions, she was mistaken. For very soon after the wedding her health seemed poor. She was nervous and curiously ill-tempered for a new bride. No wonder. All her accomplices were starting to blackmail her. She now lived in dread that she would be found out.

Somerset himself seemed to be out of favour with the King, who had grown rather tired of his favourites's overbearing manner and was tending to prefer George Villiers, who was to become Duke of Buckingham. There was nothing he could do to stop Villier's rapid advancement and his enemies scented blood.

In the autumn of 1615 when Frances had been married for two years William Reeve, who had given Sir Thomas Overbury the fatal dose of poison, fell dangerously ill and began worrying about the fate of his immortal soul. He unburdened himself of his guilty secret and recovered.

The facts were eventually laid before the King who gave orders that justice must be done. Somerset and his Countess were told not to leave their apartments until a preliminary hearing had been held. Gradually the whole story came out, and both of them were arrested on a charge of murder.

From the beginning Somerset protested that he knew nothing of the murder of his friend and stood firm in his denial right to the end. He was sentenced to death but there was a general wish that the King should spare his life and at the twelfth hour he was granted a pardon. On the other hand, feeling ran high against the Countess and at one stage it was thought likely that she would have to submit to the death penalty pronounced in court. The King granted her a pardon, on the grounds that her family had done the country so much good service and that she had sworn to be truly penitent. But there were demonstrations against her in the streets and one day a mob attacked a coach in which the Queen was travelling with a young friend. They had made the mistake of thinking it was 'that vile woman' and her mother.

Robert Devereux, Earl of Essex

Both Frances and Somerset were imprisoned in the Tower. She pleaded with the lieutenant not to put her in the room where Overbury had died. They stayed there until January 1621 when the King allowed them to go to Grey's Court in Oxfordshire where Lord Wallingford, brother-in-law of Frances, had offered them accommodation. The only condition was they were never to leave. They were under house arrest for the rest of their lives.

The punishment was worse than anybody could have dreamed. Somerset loathed the woman who had brought about his downfall and disgrace, turned him against his friend and then had that friend cruelly murdered. He hardly ever spoke to her again. Day in, day out they were forced together in an intimacy that was sheer torture. And when Frances died from a terrible wasting disease in August 1632 the last thing she saw was the contempt in his eyes.

Belle Gunness

There was only one name they could give to Mrs Belle Gunness and that was 'The female Bluebeard'. How else could you described a woman who had coldly and systematically murdered at least 100 people?

To her neighbours she had seemed pleasant enough. She was a widow and ran a small but successful farm in the green hills of La Porte County, Indiana, USA. There was something a bit foreign about her and perhaps she was a bit flighty but that did not mean to say she was not hard working and respectable.

They were terribly shocked when they heard one morning in April 1908 that there had been a terrible fire at the Gunness farm during the night and the comely widow and her three young children had been burned to death in the flames.

But they were even more shocked when the police arrived and started digging up the farmstead and excavating the fields, finding graves and corpses everywhere they looked.

The truth might not have come out for years but someone remembered that a farm hand named Lamphere, who had worked for Mrs Gunness for years, had left the farm suddenly a day or so before the fire. He was thought to have had some grievance against her and would mutter threats when he had had too many beers in the local bar.

Following up this clue the police managed to track down Lamphere and subjected him to continual and intense questioning. He broke down under it and confessed that he had killed his employer and her children with an axe while they slept and had set fire to the farmhouse to destroy the evidence of what he had done.

Why did he do it? 'I had to' he exclaimed. 'If I hadn't killed her, she would have killed me. I knew too much'.

'Knew too much? How do you mean?' asked the policeman in charge of the case.

'The woman was a murderess. She killed people they way you and me would kill rabbits.'

Hardly able to believe what he was hearing, the policeman asked softly 'How did she kill them?'

'With an axe, after she'd chloroformed them' groaned Lamphere. 'She buried them on the farm.'

For weeks following his confession, the Gunness farm was full of grim faced men, digging. Bodies of men, women and children were found neatly interred, mostly in separate graves, but sometimes two buried together. Beneath the cement floor of the farmhouse they found a deep pit full of human bones. Belle Gunness must have been at work for years, filling her own private cemetery.

Eventually the whole story was pieced together and it chilled the blood of even those used to dealing with murder. The scale of her wickedness was beyond anything they had come across.

She was Norwegian by birth and had emigrated to America as a girl. While still in her teens she had met and married a Swede called Albert Sorenson. She poisoned him in 1900 after having insured him for a tidy sum.

With this money she bought the farm in Indiana, and thinking she needed a man about the place to do the heavy work, married Joe Gunness. There was some evidence that she was already deeply involved with a murderer named Hoch whose speciality was advertising for wives then killing them off for their money. Some of these unfortunate women were sent to stay with Mrs Gunness and never heard of again. Her husband must have tumbled onto her secret and was killed with an axe one night to make sure he didn't talk. The man Hoch was arrested and executed and she decided from that time she would operate on her own.

The only difference was, she advertised for husbands.

She inserted the same notice in small provincial papers all over the United States. It read as follows:

'PERSONAL – Comely widow, who owns large farm in one of the finest districts of La Porte County, Indiana, desires to make the acquaintance of a gentleman unusually well provided, with a view to joining fortunes. No replies by letter will be considered unless the sender is willing to follow an answer with a personal visit.'

Whether they were attracted by the thought of the comely widow or by her fortune makes no difference. Gentlemen replied to her advertisements with alacrity – scores of them. She could pick and choose her victims, telling them to bring substantial sums of ready cash with them when they came to inspect the farm, just so that she could be sure of their good faith.

One by one they fell into her trap. The prospective husband would be received with open arms, shown round the farm, then, when he had eaten a huge farmhouse supper he would be shown into her guest room. It was really a death cell. The bed was comfortable enough but the thick oak door was fastened with a spring lock, the windows had iron bars and the walls were of double thickness, the cavity packed with sawdust, making the room completely sound proof. First there would be the chloroform, then she would kill with an axe. She had got the routine down to a fine art.

She had the skill of a siren when it came to those who did not respond quickly enough to her initial overture. This is a letter which was sent to a man called Andrew Helgelein in December 1907:

'To the dearest friend in all the world – I know you have now only to come to me and be my own. The king will be no happier than you when you get here. As for the queen, her joy will be small when compared with mine. You will love my farm, sweetheart. In all La Porte County, there's none will compare with it. It is on a nice green slope near two lakes. When I hear your name mentioned, my heart beats in wild rapture for you. My Andrew, I love you!'

At the bottom of the page she had scrawled 'Be sure and bring the three thousand dollars you are going to invest in the farm with you and, for safety's sake, sew them up in your clothes, dearest.'

Andrew Helgelein visited Mrs Gunness. He was seen by some neighbours as she drove him in her pony and trap towards the farm. But he never came out again.

As her lust for money and possessions grew, she killed more frequently. Sometimes whole families were wiped out. It had always been presumed they had left the district hurriedly until they were discovered in their graves. Something of the sort happened on Christmas Day 1906. Mrs Gunness invited two married women she knew who wore particularly fine jewels. She told them to bring their husbands along to the farm and help a lonely widow celebrate the festive season. As she had anticipated, they came wearing all their best trinkets. By Boxing Day not one of them was left alive and all four were identified when they were found by the police.

Exactly how many people she murdered was never known. The authorities could only make estimates with the help of the imprisoned Lamphere, who had made a long confession. He said she had carried on her foul trade for roughly five years and that she averaged three victims a month. His estimate was thought to be exaggerated. Still, even allowing for that, the police found that by adding on the victims of other murders she was known to have committed outside the farm, the total must be well over one hundred.

Why did no one suspect her before? It appears there had been inquiries about some of the men who disappeared after visiting her at the farm and Andrew Helgelein's brother was about to start an investigation at the time of the fire.

But after all, she seemed such a nice women and the farm was so well run. No one accused her and if a farmhand called Lamphere had not set fire to the place, she might have gone on for years.

Chicago May

Her real name was Mary Vivienne Churchill. She wafted through the foyers of the world's great hotels in *crêpe de chine* and pearls, a vision of loveliness with her spun gold hair, green eyes and white satin skin. Men were captivated by her, willingly became entangled with her, only to find that one morning when they awoke she had turned on them with the venom of a rattlesnake, demanding more money than they dared to think of.

She was known to the police as Chicago May, a leading member of the underworld and one of the most vicious blackmailers of modern times. Her one object in life was to make as much money as possible and, using the bedroom as her centre of operations, she bled her victims white.

Born in Ireland, the daughter of respectable, well-off parents, she was thought to have 'a bit of a devil' in her as a child, but nothing to worry about. By the age of 16 she had turned into a beauty and began to show her true colours. With cool calculation, she threw herself at the son of a leading Irish family, seduced him, then threatened to tell his parents if he didn't pay her handsomely to keep her mouth shut. The young man paid up, but she told them nevertheless. To get rid of her they gave in to her demands: a thousand pounds and a passage to America.

It was 1912, still a decade before Al Capone, but the underworld was bristling with gangsters, hoodlums and big time grafters. May dressed herself in the height of fashion and headed straight for Chicago. Before she was 20 she had been accepted into the fraternity as a high class operator.

Her victims were mostly very rich men in their fifties or sixties, tycoons, heads of industry, public figures and bored husbands all on the look out for a beautiful woman to flatter them and on whom they could spend their hard earned money. Her technique was simple. She would use her considerable charm to enslave some hapless male, modestly accept his homage of jewellery and cash, then allow herself to be seduced. Before he knew what was happening incriminating photographs had been produced, threats made and his reputation put up for sale.

As a result of these tactics Chicago May could soon afford a splendid house with servants, her own personal bodyguard and a film star wardrobe. Then, at the height of her success, she met the criminal Eddie Guerin, a tough, unscrupulous bank robber with flinty blue eyes and a chilling presence. They seemed made for each other. They became lovers and he dominated the rest of her life. Eddie had no squeamish feelings about May sleeping with rich men. That was business. But if she showed any sign of being attracted to someone nearer her own age, he turned very nasty indeed.

Her reign in Chicago lasted for about four years during which time she was estimated to have gained over half a million dollars by blackmail. Her victims' lives were never the same again, even after they had paid their dues. The head of one huge steel combine went straight to the police, only to find that the high ranking officer to whom he complained was already in her pay. Another threatened to shoot her but was frightened off by her henchmen. One younger man she had seduced then bled to the point of ruin, killed himself.

Just when she was at the height of her career in Chicago, the Press decided to run a series of exposure articles that would involve not only some very distinguished citizens but also her part in their corrupt goings on. She was told to quit before something unpleasant happened to her.

May felt that what she had done in Chicago she could do anywhere else. She packed up her sables and headed for New York. Eddie followed in a very short time. But as she drifted round the luxury hotels, planning her campaign, she began to have an unpleasant feeling that things were not going to work out. The social scene in New York was entirely different. She had no contacts. And the top criminals, sensing that she spelled trouble, didn't want to know her. The police, having been warned by their colleagues in Chicago hinted that they had enough evidence to put her away for a long stretch. It was all going wrong. May decided there was only one thing to do. She had to return to Europe.

She started her tour of the major European cities in high style. Booking herself into the most expensive and fashionable hotels she performed her old routine and, for a year or two, tasted something of her old success. In Berlin she managed to separate a great industrialist from a quarter of a million marks. In Vienna she compromised a prince of a royal house and the family paid a huge sum to get her out of their lives. It was the sort of thing she thrived on.

Eventually she crossed the Channel to London, booked into a luxury hotel and prepared to start work. London was not as easy as she had expected. The British male, she found, was far more reticent, more suspicious than his counterpart in America or on the Continent. She made a few minor conquests but had to admit to herself that she had failed. Was it anything to do with the fact that too many late nights and too much brandy had coarsened her skin, left pouches under her eyes and added an inch or two to her exquisite figure?

With great relief she heard that her old lover Eddie Guerin had arrived in Paris and wanted her to join him. She found him staying in seedy lodgings in Montmartre, planning the biggest job of his criminal life. He was going to break into the strong room of the American Express Company. After that, he promised her, they could both retire.

The night that Eddie and his gang blew the safes and brought out nearly half a million dollars in American currency, May was standing on a street corner, playing the uncharacteristic role of look out. She wouldn't have done it for any other man. The money had to be moved out of the country without delay. Every minute counted. The gang split up and began swiftly to put their plan into operation. But they were not quick enough. An informer gave the French police two names: Eddie and Chicago May. They were picked up as they were packing their suitcases with dollars.

Eddie knew he was finished but when May denied she had taken any part in the raid he backed her up. The French police were pretty sure she had been an accomplice but they let her go, content that they had managed to capture one of the most dangerous bank robbers in the world. But May loved Eddie. Though she had managed to escape to London she couldn't bear to think she might not see him for years. She returned to Paris to see him in prison before his trial and this time the French authorities pounced. She was sentenced to five years imprisonment for her part in the robbery. She nearly collapsed when she heard that Eddie had been sent to the dreaded French penal colony on Devil's Island for life.

When she came out of prison she had to face the fact that her beauty was fading fast. The sort of life she had led was etched on her face. Back in London she set up her own organisation: the Northumberland Avenue Gang. She was deep into blackmail again but this time using prostitutes. It was a lucrative but dangerous racket and, to her cost, May found that the police in London were not, on the whole, open to corruption. When the law caught up with the Northumberland Avenue Gang many of its members were arrested but May managed to slip through a back door and lie low.

Next time she surfaced, it was in another trade. With her looks no longer what they were and her gang dispersed she decided to give up blackmail. With the money she had saved she opened a plush opium den only a stone's throw from Piccadilly Circus. It became a 'must' for young male tourists who wanted to see the *real* London and soon she added a brothel as an extra attraction. As Gerald Sparrow writes in his account of her life: 'The whole thing was filthy, unsavoury and weird and attracted the dregs of humanity.'

One morning May heard a sharp knock on her front door and opened it to find Eddie Guerin standing there. The shock was almost too much for her. He had escaped from Devil's Island – in one of the greatest prison breaks ever made – and had come to find her. She still loved him but she knew how much she had changed and wondered if she could hold him.

For the first six months they were happy enough together then May started to notice any attention Eddie gave to younger women. Soon she was jealous of every female he looked at. There were violent scenes and Eddie's eyes became colder and colder. One day he vanished as suddenly as he had appeared. He had taken with him an eighteen-year-old girl who was working for her.

When May realised what had happened she went beserk. In her fury and jealousy she only knew she had to destroy him. She hired a young professional gunman and became obsessed with hunting him down. The terrible confrontation came one afternoon in a street in Bloomsbury. As soon as May saw Eddie with his girl friend she rushed at him with a knife, but the gunman shot him before she could use it. They left him sprawled on the pavement in a pool of blood with the girl sobbing over his body.

By some miracle Eddie Guerin did not die. He lost several pints of blood but the doctors pulled him through and he went on living. Chicago May was arrested in 1926 and charged with attempted murder, along with her hired gun. There was no trace left of her golden haired beauty. She sat huddled in the dock like an old woman and when they sentenced her to fifteen years she turned and left the court without saying a word.

Chapter
Eight

They Left a Question Mark

Finally there is the select band of women with notorious names who have left a question mark....

Madeleine Smith

The sensational trial of Madeleine Smith which kept staid Edinburgh in a ferment for nine days in July 1857, has always divided people into two camps. There are those who believe that Madeleine was a cunning, cold-hearted poisoner who, once she had tired of her lover, killed him so that she could marry someone socially superior. And there are those who consider her a pathetic victim of blackmail, driven to despair by Emile L'Angelier, the man she once loved, but totally innocent of his death.

When the jury returned a verdict of 'Not proven' Madeleine Smith, who, throughout the trial had shown interest, but no concern, was seen to sigh heavily, then smile. Wild cheering echoed through the court. But the fact remained that L'Angelier had died an agonising death with eighty two grains of arsenic in his stomach, enough to kill a dozen men, and nobody knew how it had got there.

Before having an opinion one way or the other it is necessary to know something about the background of this handsome, languid girl from a middle class Victorian home and her suitor, an impoverished but dapper young packing clerk who desperately wanted position and respect and 'a lady' for his wife.

Madeleine was the elder daughter of a highly successful Scottish architect, James Smith, who was one of the pillars of Glasgow. He had offices in Vincent Street, a solid family house in India Street and a somewhat over-ornate country residence on the Clyde. She was not beautiful but her lustrous eyes, luxuriant brown curls and graceful carriage made her very attractive. Her father was a typical Victorian papa who provided a prosperous household with six servants for his family, but expected his word to be taken as law. She emerged in her finery most evenings to attend some function or other but the days could be tedious with little to do but occupy herself with typical Victorian hobbies thought suitable for a young lady such as painting on vellum, making feather flowers and creating pictures from seaweed. What no one knew, until she met Emile, was that behind the facade of demure respectability was a vibrant, sensual woman crying to be let out.

Emile L'Angelier was a total stranger to her sort of world. His father was a nurseryman in Jersey and he had been sent to Scotland to work with a firm of seedmen, with the object of improving his status. When Madeleine met him, however, he was still a packing clerk, earning very little, but with rather grandiose ideas about his future. However his employer seemed to consider him industrious, honest and sober and if he was somewhat vain, perhaps that was because he was French.

She first saw him staring at her as she was strolling in Sauchiehall Street with a friend. Their eyes met, and he bowed. He discovered someone at his work who knew her and who promised he would introduce Emile at the first opportunity. When that moment came he took the opportunity of giving her a note, a *billet doux*, which expressed his feelings in flowery terms. Madeleine told him she had worn it next to her heart at the ball that night. So began the vast correspondence that was later to prove so damning. The letters showed that by April 1855 he had gained her affections but was not sure of them. Twice during the year she tried to break off their relationship but he was persistent. He made it clear he was not a man to be so easily dropped. In a copy of a letter written as early as 19 July 1855 he showed what he was capable of. 'Think what your father would say if I sent him your letters for perusal. . . .'

She had poured out all her suppressed sensuality on paper, writing him love letters that made people gasp with shock, for it was a period at which women were supposed to suffer sex, not enjoy it. Later, when L'Anglier's lodgings were searched over 500 letters from Madeleine were discovered and sixty of them were read out in court.

Their go-between was a friend of Emile's called Mary Perry who seems to have been fond of him without expecting a relationship. She was perfectly satisfied to be a letter carrier between her friend and this fine lady and let them use her house for their secret meetings.

Once they had declared their love for each other in fulsome romantic terms they became 'engaged' and obviously slept together. On 7 May 1856 Madeleine wrote him this letter:

'My own beloved husband:

I trust to God you got home safe, and were not much the worse for being out. Thank you, my love, for coming so far to see your Mimi. It is truly a pleasure to see my Emile. If we did wrong last night, it must have been in the excitement of our love. I suppose we ought to have waited till we were married. Yes, beloved, I did truly love you with my soul. I was happy; it was a pleasure to be with you. Oh, if we could have remained, never more to have parted! Darling Emile, did I seem cold to you last night? Darling, I love you, my own Emile. I love you with all my heart and soul. Am I not your wife? Yes, I am; and you may rest assured that after what has passed I cannot be the wife of any other. . . .'

Madeleine had obviously made up her mind to introduce Emile to her father, but James Smith had no intention of letting his daughter marry a penniless little foreigner. 'Do keep cool when you see him, I know his temper – every inch like my own' she advised Emile. But the meeting never took place. Emile's pride was wounded and the hurt is reflected in a letter he wrote to his beloved in which he fumes and fusses about the treatment he has received.

'Never fear my own beloved husband' she wrote to console him 'I shall be quite ready whenever you fix our marriage day. . . . I am quite sure when they hear we are married they will all give in.'

When the family moved down to Row, their country house on the Clyde she asked for a ground floor bedroom. This meant she just had to step out of her window to meet him. Throughout that summer of 1856 she abandoned herself to her love. Emile seems to have accepted that they were betrothed and that they would eventually be married.

But he had also noticed that a certain name seemed to have crept into her conversation and her letters with a frequency that alarmed him. The name was William Minnoch. This gentleman had for some time admired Madeleine and wanted her for his wife. He was a short, fair complexioned business man in his thirties, well educated, successful and well liked by James Smith who considered him an ideal son-in-law. He began calling, with obvious intent, but Madeleine said she did not find him in the least attractive and was not interested in him. 'Don't give ear to any reports you may hear . . . there are several going about regarding me getting married . . . regard them not' she told Emile. But he was very disturbed and she did not help matters when she remarked in a letter she sent him towards the end of August: 'Minnoch was never so pleasant as he has been this last visit. He was very nice indeed.'

When the Smith family returned to Glasgow secret meetings were made more difficult than before. They moved to a different house and this time Madeleine's bedroom was in the basement with the bedroom window at street level covered by bars. There was no chance of her slipping out without being detected. They would sometimes have a whispered conversation through the bars but it was not very satisfactory. Emile began to feel depressed.

Still, nothing had prepared him for the shock which came in her next letter. She talked of their love as though it was in the past. 'We shall often talk over all our past performances – it really has been quite a small romance' she said lightly. He was devastated. He began to see his dream of being someone of consequence fading rapidly as he woke to the reality of her increasing coldness towards him.

She had been seen in public with Minnoch and her letters to Emile became shorter and shorter and were signed simply 'Yours devotedly'. There was no doubt that she had enjoyed being escorted by someone as well regarded and

The trial of Madeleine Smith

socially acceptable as William, as she now called him, and on 28 January she made up her mind to accept his proposal of marriage.

First, she had to bring an end to her affair with the little Frenchman. Emile played into her hands by indulging in a petty little habit with which he showed her his displeasure. He returned one of her letters. Her response, considering the passionate abandon of her previous correspondence was brutal.

> 'This may astonish you, but you have more than once returned me my letters and my mind was made up that I should not stand the same thing again. And you also annoyed me much on Saturday by your conduct in coming so near to me. Altogether I think owing to coolness and indifference (nothing else) that we had better for the future consider ourselves as strangers. I trust to your honour as a gentleman that you will not reveal anything that has passed between us.... I shall feel obliged by your bringing me my letters and likeness.... I trust you may yet be happy, and get one more worthy of you than I.'

It became evident that he would not give her up without a fight. Nor would he give up the letters and threatened to show them to her father. His friend Tom Kennedy, who was cashier at Huggins, where he worked, tried to persuade him to behave like a gentleman and let the whole affair come to an end. Weeping, Emile told him 'No, I shan't; she shall never marry another man as long as I live...' He also said miserably 'Tom, it's an infatuation; she shall be the death of me.'

When Madeleine realized that he was not going to return the letters and might, in his present state, pluck up the courage to show them to her father she became frantic. 'Emile will you not spare me this – hate me, despise me – but do not expose me. I cannot write more. I feel ill tonight.'

She asked him to come to the house, where she could talk to him through the bedroom window. He kept the appointment on 11 February 1857 and she appears to have agreed to a wedding the following September.

On the morning of 20 February when Emile's landlady, Mrs Jenkins went to call him for breakfast, she found him very ill. He said that on the evening before as he was returning home he was seized with violent spasms in the stomach and thought he was going to die before he could reach his bed. During the night he had been very sick. Four days later Mrs Jenkins was wakened at four in the morning by groans and cries from his room. The symptons were the same as on 20 February, but this time Emile was shivering and complained that he was cold and thirsty. The doctor who was fetched to see him, decided it was a bilious attack and prescribed accordingly. He advised him to take a short holiday.

At about this time Madeleine had been shoping for arsenic in Sauchiehall Street. She went into a chemist and asked for sixpence worth of poison. Asked for what purpose she needed it she replied 'For the garden and for rats at our country house.' The arsenic was sold to her mixed with soot according to the law and she seemed concerned about the colour of it. The chemist admitted afterwards he did wonder why if she was only giving it to rats.

She had written to Emile showing concern about his bilious attacks, addressing him as 'My dear, sweet Emile' and sending him love and kisses. She assured him she loved no one else in the world but him. Emile, by now wary of her passionate outpourings, asked her to give him some plain answers to his questions. Nevertheless, he signed himself 'your ever affectionate husband – Emile L'Angelier'.

Emile was feeling a little better and went to see his friend and go-between, Miss Perry. He told her he had seen Madeleine then remarked 'I can't think why I was so unwell after getting coffee and chocolate from her on the two occasions we met.' He even went as far as to say he thought the drinks might have been poisoned, but obviously, did not consider that had anything to do with the woman he loved.

She was very much occupied elsewhere. She had gone up to Bridge of Allan in Stirlingshire to make arrangements for her marriage to William Minnoch. She seems to have forgotten that she had promised to marry Emile in September. Before she left Glasgow she had been shopping again. This time she asked for an ounce of arsenic 'for rats in Blythwood Square' (their Glasgow home). But Christina Haggart, the Smith's maid swore she had never seen a rat in that house.

Madeleine continued to write Emile affectionate letters: 'I long to see you, to kiss and embrace you, my own, only sweet love. Miss me my sweet one – my love, my own dear sweet little pet'. Why she insisted on sending him these sugary epistles while demanding the return of her other letters is hard to guess.

Emile got leave from work and caught the train to Bridge of Allan hoping to catch Madeleine but she had already returned to Glasgow. He had missed a letter she had written asking him to meet her on 19 March and another letter containing an urgent summons was sent on to him by his landlady. He read the note eagerly: 'Why, my beloved, did you not come to me. Oh beloved are you ill? Come to me sweet one. I waited and waited for you, but you care not. I shall wait again tomorrow night same hour and arrangement. Do come sweet love, my own dear love of a sweetheart. . . .' He caught the first train back.

When he arrived back at his lodgings in Franklin Place on the evening of 22 March he told his landlady that he would be very late that night. He went out, presumably to see Madeleine. He did not return until half past two in the morning and rang the bell violently. Mrs Jenkins found him doubled up with pain on the doorstep. He told her all the old symptons had returned and she helped him to his room where he again vomited a greenish substance. By four in the morning he was so bad Mrs Jenkins herself ran out to fetch the doctor, who said he would visit him in the morning, meanwhile she was to give him a few drops of laudanum and a mustard plaster. But two hours later in response to urgent pleas from Mrs Jenkins he stirred himself and hurried round to Franklin Place to give his patient a morphine injection.

When Mrs Jenkins drew back the curtains in Emile's room at nine o'clock the next morning he looked so pale that she asked if he would care to see anybody. He asked for his friend, Miss Perry, but before she could be fetched the doctor arrived. When he lifted Emile's head from the pillow, it fell back limply. He was dead.

When they came to look through his belongings they found a letter which began 'Why, my beloved, did you not come to me? . . . '

Nothing now could stop the relentless stream of inquiries and of course they led straight to Madeleine, to her love affair with Emile and to the letters she had written him. An autopsy had revealed that Emile's stomach had contained enough arsenic to kill 40 men and the position of the poison in his body showed that it had been ministered more than once.

One morning when the maid servant went to waken Madeleine, she found her bed empty. It was thought that she had probably gone to their country house and Minnoch set off with one of her brothers to fetch her back. They caught up with her on the Clyde steamer but the tactful husband to be asked for no explanations.

On Tuesday 31 March Madeleine, showing great composure, made a statement to the Sheriff of Lanarkshire telling the whole story of her relationship with Emile L'Angelier and even admitting that they had plans to marry. But she insisted the last time she saw him was three weeks before his death.

When the trial began on 30 June all eyes were fixed on the trapdoor leading down to the cells. There was a gasp from the public gallery as the prisoner came up and moved towards the dock. She was tall, elegantly dressed with a fashionable bonnet, and exuded an air of nonchalance that some observers thought indecent. She was veiled and carried a lace edged handkerchief and a bottle of smelling salts. She rose, threw back her veil and in a clear voice declared herself 'Not Guilty'.

She was asked why she had bought arsenic and, contrary to what she had told the chemist she explained to the court that it was purely for cosmetic purposes, to soften her hands and improve her complexion. Victorian women often did this, though it was obviously unwise. Madeleine said she had diluted it with water and used it on her face, neck and arms. The prosecution made a great deal of the fact that she had given one reason for purchasing arsenic to the Glasgow chemist but quite a different one to the court. It was however essential to show that she had arsenic at the right time and also the opportunity for administering it at that time. Could she have laced the coffee and cocoa she handed to Emile through her bedroom window? It was very hard to prove.

On the fifth day of her trial the letters were produced and read out in a thin voice by the aged clerk. The Lord Advocate ordered that passages that were particularly offensive should be omitted. She did not show a scrap of emotion as she heard evidence of her passionate love for the dead man.

When it came to the summing up the Lord Advocate for the prosecution, said he would show that Madeleine had got herself into such a position that murder was the only solution. She had, he said, the means, the opportunity, the motive and the cool character that was perfectly compatible with murder. But Dean Inglis of the Faculty of Advocates, for the defence, put Madeleine's case in a masterly speech. He presented Emile as vain, pretentious and conceited, a seducer who had corrupted an innocent girl. He had also at one time boasted of being an arsenic eater and there was evidence he had been a frequent sufferer from stomach ailments. 'Think you' the Dean demanded 'that without temptation, without evil teaching, a poor girl falls into such depths of degredation? No! Influence from without – most corrupting influence – can alone account for such a fall.' He appealed to the noblest instincts of all those listening to consider the awful fate of this girl if found guilty.

The jury was out for 25 minutes before bringing in their 'Not Proven' verdict. It may have been popular with the crowds but it was noticed that the usually courteous Dean Inglis left the courtroom without so much as a glance at his client. Only when it was all over did they begin to think of her total lack of emotion. One newspaper commented that she had demeaned herself as if L'Angelier had never had a place in her affections. 'If it had been a trial for poisoning a dog, the indifference could not have been greater.'

Her indifference towards William Minnoch was equally noticeable. The whole business had made him ill with grief but when told he had been ill she commented 'My friend I know nothing of. I have not seen him. I hear he has been ill, which I don't much care.' Minnoch had had to make a very brief appearance as a witness for the prosecution and was never forgiven.

The 'Not proven' verdict was not a comfortable one to live with in Scotland. It really meant that some parts of the evidence were too doubtful to risk a conviction. Madeleine moved to London where she married an artist, bore him three children and lived an interesting life. Her last days were spent in America where she died at the great age of 91, protesting her innocence to the end.

Lucrezia Borgia

Lucrezia Borgia is, of course, the name on everyone's lips when you mention the subject of wicked women. She belonged to one of the most feared and hated families in history and the unspeakable crimes laid at her door include incest, not only with her brother, Cesare, but with her father, Pope Alexander VI.

The Borgias were certainly a terrible brood, but does Lucrezia herself deserve the reputation she has gained over the centuries?

Those who have written about her in modern times have come to the conclusion that she was used as a pawn by the brilliant, ruthless, Borgia men and sacrificed to their terrible ambition. It was under their influence and through their actions that she became 'the most execrated woman of her age'.

She lived in a world in which the concepts of decency and morality were very different from our own. The fact that her father, the libertine Rodrigo Borgia, could become head of the Catholic Church was evidence of that. But, says the historian Gregorovius, who is the most quoted authority on Lucrezia, 'she was neither better nor worse than the women of her time. She was thoughtless and filled with the joy of living'.

If she had not been the daughter of Alexander VI and the sister of Cesare Borgia she would have been unnoticed by the historians of her age, or at most would have been mentioned only as one of the many charming women who constituted the society of Rome. In the hands of her father and her brother, however, she became the tool and also the victim of their political machinations, against which she had not the strength to make any resistance.

Chroniclers of the day using scandal, innuendo and rumour, and the very real hatred felt for the Borgias, turned Lucrezia into a legendary monster and that is the picture that has endured.

Her family, Spanish in origin, had a meteoric rise from obscurity because within a relatively short span of time it produced a number of brilliant men, distinguished by their sensual beauty, force of intellect and ruthless ambition.

One of these was Cardinal Rodrigo Borgia whose mistress, a Roman beauty called Vannozza, bore him several children including Lucrezia and the infamous Cesare.

Lucrezia was born on 18 April 1480. She was brought up in her mother's house on the Piazza Pizzo di Merlo, only a few steps away from the Cardinal's Palace. Rodrigo did not acknowledge the children as his own until he had been made pope and was absolutely sure of his power.

Before she was eleven years old the first suitor had made a bid for Lucrezia's hand. Two months later another appeared and was favourably considered, but both were swept away as too insignificant when Rodrigo took the Triple Crown and desired a prestigious match for his lovely daughter.

He put her into the care of the two women who were closest to him, his cousin and confidante Adriana di Mila, who was married to an Orsini, and her daughter-in-law Giulia Farnese, an exquisite woman, said to be a poem in gold and ivory, who became Rodrigo's most famous mistress. These two tended the darling of the Borgia family like a hot-house orchid, keeping her apart in the splendour of the Palazzo of Santa Maria until she was prepared for her first marriage.

At thirteen Lucrezia was golden-haired and graceful, with a slender white neck and teeth like pearls; a delectable morsel to offer to the handsome Giovanni Sforza, Lord of Pesare. They were married in a magnificent ceremony to which half of Rome was invited.

The marriage was not to last long. The Borgias saw to that. They soon realised they had underplayed their hand in marrying Lucrezia to Sforza when they could have used her to gain entrance to the powerful house of Aragon. They made up their minds to get rid of the unfortunate bridegroom.

Their method could not have been more humiliating. They announced to the world that Sforza had proved impotent and that his wife was still a virgin. The greviously insulted Lord of Pesaro called upon all the saints in the calender to bear witness that he was a full man and had 'known his wife carnally on countless occasions'. Ripped from the arms of the child-wife he loved, he swore vengeance on the Borgias. But their power was too great. They forced him to sign a confession admitting his impotence and he fled Rome before anything worse could happen to him.

Although Lucrezia had not been averse to this first husband, she accepted the family decision without protest and retired to the convent of San Sisto on the Via Appia to enhance her virginal image in preparation for another marriage. When she left the convent the nuns were said to have been loathe to see her go for she had turned the convent into a place of sophistication and fashionable pleasure.

Towards the end of February 1498 news spread through Rome that

THE WORLD'S WICKEDEST WOMEN

Lucrezia was pregnant. Her lover, it was said, was a Spanish gentleman at the Papal Court; Pedro Calderon, known generally as Perotto. A man of immense charm, he was certainly guilty of desiring her, if not actually seducing her. Cesare Borgia had Perotto thrown into prison and soon after his corpse was found in the river Tiber.

From this affair stemmed most of the stories of incest that hung like a foul miasma about the Borgias for ever after. Cesare, a dazzling man, handsome, hard and pitiless, certainly loved his sister with an intensity that seemed abnormal and could have been incestuous in motive although there is no evidence that her affection for him was of the same nature. Rumours began to spread that the child Lucrezia was said to be expecting was the result of incest. Sforza seized upon the gossip to get his own back and accused Lucrezia of sleeping not only with her brother but with her father, the pope.

Whatever the truth – and Perotto was the most likely father – a child called Giovanni, who was later created Duke of Nepi, was born in Rome on March 1498. He grew up at Lucrezia's side but she always referred to him as her little brother. By others he was referred to enigmatically as 'The Roman Infante'. He remained a mystery.

The next match arranged for Lucrezia was, like the first, for political reasons. Alfonso, nephew of the King of Naples who created him Duke of Bisceglie for the alliance, was however, of far more use to the Borgias than poor Sforza. Through him Cesare hoped to gain entrance by marriage to the house of Aragon.

All the omens were good. When Lucrezia first set eyes on the fair, incredibly good looking Duke she was immediately won over. Although their marriage had been so coldly arranged, it was obviously going to be a love match. Cesare Borgia greeted him with signs of great friendship and when the wedding took place six days after his arrival in Rome, no expense was spared to make it an occasion of great splendour.

Alfonso promised to stay in Rome with Lucrezia for one year before carrying her off to his lands near the sea, and all seemed well until the blood-thirsty Cesare started his political intriguing once again. Before long he and the young bridegroom were at daggers drawn. Many in Rome saw the terrible signs of Cesare's jealousy and said prayers for the Duke of Bisceglie.

One evening Alfonso visited the Vatican. When he set out from there to make his way home to the Palace of Santa Maria, across the Piazza of St Peter's he was brutally attacked. His friends carried him home half dead with a split skull and terrible wounds to his body and legs. When Lucrezia saw him she nearly fainted. She nursed Alfonso back to health with great devotion but Cesare was determined to finish the job that had been so badly bungled.

One evening as Alfonso rested at home, a gang of ruffians broke into his

Lucrezia Borgia

room and one of them, a professional garrotter, killed him before he could cry for help. The affair marked a new phase in Cesare's career in ruthlessness and no one heeded his protests that the Duke of Bisceglie had threatened him.

Lucrezia was sent away from Rome to the Castle of Nepi where, for a time, she cried bitterly over the loss of her beautiful young husband. But she was a Borgia and in spite of her tenderness for the dead Alfonso, she dried her tears and waited to see what her father and brothers had in store for her next.

Recalled to the Vatican by her father, Lucrezia tried to amuse herself, in spite of being a widow. Lurid accounts were printed of the parties which Cesare gave to distract her. At one of these he was said to have strewn hot chestnuts over the floor of the pope's apartment and forced naked courtesans to crawl along lighted candles to retrieve them. Other accounts of parties at which prizes were awarded in fertility contests and obscene theatricals were performed, reminded many people of earlier Roman orgies.

There is no record of Lucrezia ever taking part, however. Indeed about this time she began to be better known for her piety and gentleness.

She was about to be introduced to her third husband. The Borgias had chosen an alliance with the ancient and noble family of d'Este but negotiations had not gone as smoothly as they wished. Their prospective bridegroom, Alfonso d'Esta, the Duke of Ferrara's son, balked at the prospect of taking to his bed a lady of such notoriety. He was also worried that he might suffer the same fate as her previous husband. His father, furious that his plans for the alliance were in jeopardy, warned his son that he would marry Lucrezia himself if neccessary.

The two families argued and bargained and eventually the Pope settled a fabulous dowry on his daughter. Even so, it was only half of that demanded. Lucrezia was married for the third time in great splendour and at her wedding was seen to dance radiantly with the brother who had made her a widow.

She took leave of her father for the last time and set out with her new husband and a priceless trousseau including magnificent clothes, great works of art, jewellery and rare furniture to spend the rest of her days with the great Prince of Ferrara. He took her to the family's vast medieval castle at Vecchio where she continued to amaze him with her charm, grace and modesty.

For a time she continued to be a subject of gossip and speculation. Her name was linked with that of the poet, Pietro Bembo. Did she become his mistress or not? His poetry was widely believed to have been written in memory of the passionate hours he had spent in her arms. More dangerous was the friendship she cultivated with Ercole Strozzi, a fervent, elegant young poet who did not bother to hide his feelings for her.

There was a terrible scandal when Strozzi was found dead in the street, wrapped in a cloak, his body a mass of dagger wounds. Those who hated the very name of Borgia said she had organized the killing out of jealousy because the poet was about to take a wife. Others hinted that Strozzi knew too much and she had feared he might talk about the favours bestowed upon himself and Bembo by the Prince of Ferrara's wife.

Time passed, she became Duchess of Ferrara and poets and men of letters began to superimpose another image on Lucrezia, that of a supremely virtuous woman, flawless, perfect and angel of mercy. It was probably just as exaggerated as the one she had left behind in Rome.

All we do know for certain is that when she died of childbirth in June 1519 she was regarded with admiration and esteem by those who knew her. She was deeply mourned by the Duke of Ferrara who called her 'my dearest wife'.